A Black Man's Guide to Law Enforcement in America

Disclaimer: The information listed is this book is intended to be used as a guide for dealing with basic encounters with American Law Enforcement Officers. Readers should consult with an attorney if ever they are arrested, and should not rely solely on the information contained in this book.

Published by Wheatmark®
610 East Delano Street, Suite 104
Tucson, Arizona 85705 U.S.A.
www.wheatmark.com

International Standard Book Number: 978-1-60494-387-0
Library of Congress Control Number: 2009943631

rev01072010

Dedicated to Malik Jones and his Family,

Aqhmed Amadu Diallo and his Family,

And Sean Bell and his Family.

Opening

Some cops don't stop at red lights?

Do cops sleep?

After having harassed

My grandfathers, my father,

My brother, and now me.

Do cops sleep in separate rooms than their spouses?

Because they know that the next crack head they may bust

Isn't the man on the Avenue. but someone in their own family?

I'm just wondering.

When I'm waiting at the bus stop,

And they ask me what I'm doing –

Maybe they just can't see

That every young Black Man on the corner isn't selling weed.

Do cops sleep normally or maybe hanging upside down like bats?

After flying around in their cars blindly,

Chasing me,

Like I match the description of a person who just committed a felony.

Do cops sleep at all?

After they let an innocent boy take the fall,

For a crime he didn't commit,

And they knew the charge wasn't legit.

But with him the charges would stick.

Just thinking about it makes me sick!

I'm willing to admit that cops do some good,

Doesn't it seem obvious that they should?

Do cops sleep at all?

Or do they stop at red lights.

Table of Contents

Table of Contents

Acknowledgments

Mubarakah Ibrahim
C0-Editor Chip Croft, Executive Producer, Sea-TV
C0-Editor Paul Bass, Editor, New Haven Independent
C0-Editor Bonnie Posick
Co-Editor Cindy Smith
Co-Editor Sharon Bradford
Almena & Fred Fulcher
Brenda L. Fulcher & Eugene Johnson
Khaliah Abdussabur
Fred Fulcher Jr.
Bernard Fulcher
Monica Lawrence & Andre Johnson
Willian Groomes
Clinton Smith aka *Kazz*

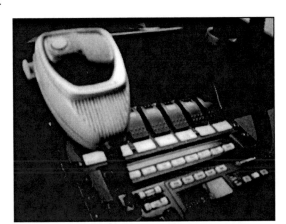

Former New Haven Police Chief Nicholas Pastore
Former New Haven Police Chief Francisco Ortiz
Hartford Police Chief Daryl Roberts
New Haven Police Chief James Lewis
Yale University Police Chief Perrotti
Yale University Assistant Chief Ronnell Higgs-Yale University Police
Former New Haven Police Chief Melvin H. Wearing
Dr. James Welbourne, Director, New Haven Public Library
The Members of the New Haven Police Department
National Association of Black Law Enforcement Officers
Charles Wilson, President NABLEO
Officer John Lali (I saved his life in 1999. More on that in the my next book)
Detective Craig Alston
Sergeant Sam Brown
Sergeant Joe Dease Jr.
Lieutenant Holly Wasilewski
Lieutenant Petisia Adger
CTRIBAT Institute For Social Development Inc.
Yale University Office Of New Haven and State Affairs
Tracey Meares Yale University Law School
Elliot Spector
Special Thanks to Emma Jones (Mother of Malik Jones)
Special Thanks to Dr. Jimmy Jones (Father of Malik Jones)
The Malik Organization Inc.
Barbara Fair, People Against Injustice

Lesson 1: Instant Nolle

How to Survive the Common Motor Vehicle Arrests

Misdemeanor Motor Vehicle Arrest

The number one cause of anxiety among young African American and Latino/Hispanic males is motor vehicle-related incidents. So frequent is its controversy, many have termed the incidents as "DWB" (Driving While Black) or racial profiling. And though there are countless opinions on this subject, the bottom line is that, in the majority of the motor vehicle stops involving Blacks and Latinos/Hispanics, the outcome is usually an arrest of some

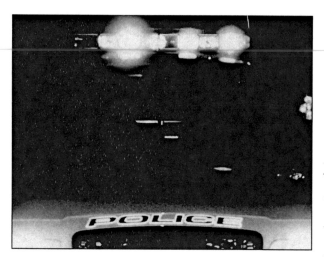

sort. That arrest is usually an infraction ticket, a misdemeanor arrest, or a custodial arrest. The irony is that, in most cases, these young men are arrested for charges that have nothing to do with motor vehicle violations but everything to do with them

not knowing how to strategically use proper citizen conduct when dealing with the police.

So let's get started. Here are the **top three reasons why most young African American and Latino/Hispanic males are stopped** or pulled over when operating a motor vehicle:

1. **Driving a car loaded down (carrying three or four males)**
2. **Driving a car with dark, tinted windows**
3. **Driving a beat-up car**

I know this from my own personal experience on and off of the job. In addition, I have discussed this topic at length with other police officers from around the country. In all three instances, these vehicles would appear suspicious in nature to almost all police officers because of the race or ethnicity of the person operating the vehicle. As a result of this bias perception, the majority of motor vehicle stops that are conducted involving African American and Latino/Hispanic males are most often initiated as criminal investigation stops. Unlike being stopped for speeding or a basic seat belt violation, young African American and Latino/Hispanic males, because of how they have been perceived by the American public, are almost always the targets of criminal investigations.

> ....the majority of motor vehicle stops that are conducted involving African American and Latino/Hispanic males are initiated as criminal investigation stops.

In law enforcement there is a term, investigative detention that is often used to better define the length of time a person can be detained during a motor vehicle stop. If you don't understand the significance to this procedure, understand this: the more time you spend in police custody, the more time you have to make a mistake that may get you locked up, increase your chances of getting a ticket, or insure that you are detained even longer. The reason I make this declaration goes back to my initial observation that, unfortunately, the average young African American and Latino/Hispanic male already has a difficult time verbally interacting with police officers. And because they lack those basic interpersonal skills, they are bound to say or do something that feeds into the officer's investigative agenda. There is a saying among officers, "If a person talks long enough, they will eventually say something that will get them locked up!"

In many other cases, if you ask a police officer what is their number one frustration on the job, they will respond with "motor vehicle arrest." I know from personal experience on the job. The biggest issue with young African American and Latino/Hispanic males is driving with what I call **The Three No's:**

- **1-No license**
- **2-No registration**
- **3-No insurance**

This is more prevalent among young African American and Latino/Hispanic males because they live in urban areas of cities where the cost of living presents challenges, especially for a young minority male who may be using summer job money to purchase clothes or to pay for college tuition. In some cases, these young men may even be contributing to the general household or to a household where the parent does not have the economic resources or the time to manage and oversee their child's involvement with a motor vehicle. Thus, you have a young African American and Latino/Hispanic male driving a car with the Three No's.

Having grown up in the urban sector as an at-risk youth, I wholeheartedly can relate to this situation. Number one, most often a young male is under a lot of pressure by young females and male peers to have transportation. Driving is freedom and freedom is empowerment. Often, when young African American and Latino/Hispanic males are pulled over with these specific motor vehicle violations, they do not necessarily see it as a crime or a violation of the law. To them it's more like an inconvenience.

The Arrest

So what do you do once you are stopped and the police begin their investigation? Well, the vast majority of the time you are going to at least get an infraction ticket, which is basically like an expensive parking ticket. In the classic case of the Three No's, in some states you will get a custodial arrest in which you will be taken to a jail cell or detention facility. In some other states, you may just receive a misdemeanor summons with a PTA (Promise to Appear in court) within a 30-day period. However, in some states, if you are a non-resident, they will give you a court date within a 24-hour period that would force you to stay in that state for another day. In such a case, it would be an obvious inconvenience but a necessary evil. So, I would strongly recommend that you stay in town and go to court.

The Uninsured Car

In some cases in which your car is uninsured, the state mandates that the officer have it towed and you not drive it. (It could become a liability on the municipality, city or state to allow you to drive an uninsured vehicle if it were to cause injury to someone, and there would be no way for the victim to be compensated). In some states, such as Connecticut, if you request it, the officer may even allow you to have the car towed to your home or residence. However, you must pay for the towing charges. This is obviously a courtesy on the officer's behalf, and they do not have to honor your request. I can tell you that if the motor vehicle stop was a *headache stop* for the officer, and you insisted on being an Al Sharpton, then you can best believe that the car is going to be towed to the designated garage.

The Court Case

So now you have been arrested, your car has been towed, and you are either waiting for a court date or appearing at a court hearing. Either way, the next suggested course of action would apply to both.

If you have a license, if your license has been suspended, or if you just don't plain have one, you should ask the Judge, prosecutor or clerk for a continuance. A continuance is a request that can be made in which they would postpone or delay your court appearance for another day. In most cases, it is a rescheduled court date of two to four weeks in the future. However, that can vary based on the jurisdiction of the court system. In a major city like New York, a motor vehicle court date could be automatically 30 days from the date of arrest.

Reasons continuances are often granted:

- Need time to hire a lawyer or attorney
- Need time to gather documents to prove innocence
- Generally not prepared to make a plea due to the above

If you are denied or think you will be denied immediately, consult with a lawyer. In most cases, if it's a basic motor vehicle violation case, many law firms will give you free over-the-phone advice. If you are fortunate to get the continuance, I suggest the next course of action. First, start thinking like a lawyer. Watch Judge Joe Mathis. He can give you some tips on <u>how not to</u> make yourself look stupid in court. Remember, motor vehicle court, as it is called in some areas, is similar to the court setting and procedures seen on Judge Judy's *"Peoples Court."* So what I am saying is that it will not hurt you to attempt to prepare yourself with proper court etiquette.

Next, you have to go out to Office Max or Staples and buy yourself a file folder or a portfolio book, like the ones lawyers and business people use. This will become your official case file. Get a nice pen. It does not have to be a Cross pen, but a knock-off version will do. This will become your case pen. Once you have done that, you will be ready for the next step.

I emphasize that the above-mentioned to-do's should be done immediately after you are released from jail, court, or in a situation in which you have a 30-day window. Don't play around with this stuff! You can probably buy all of these items on the way home from court or jail.

Even if you have to borrow the money to buy your portfolio materials, it is better to owe your friend and be free. The other option is to owe the state jail time.

Now if, for some reason, you cannot afford a portfolio ($5-$20), just get a manila folder. Label it with your docket number and court date and your name and use that. You can just write your information about the case on copy paper.

Fixing the License

Within the first 24 hours, my suggestion is that you explore doing the following. If you have:

- **No license (never had one)** — immediately contact the Department of Motor Vehicles and make a driver's test appointment. Make sure you get an official print-out of the test date, if possible. If you can, make sure that you get the name of the clerk or staff member whom you spoke with on the phone and their position. Write down the date and time you spoke with them. Write down the date and time for your test. All of this information should be put in your new case file portfolio.

- **A suspended license** — immediately contact the Department of Motor Vehicles during their normal business hours. You can also go on-line and find out their hours of operation. It's OK to leave a message, but that will not absolve you from blame should they not call you back. Some states have created a Department of Motor Vehicle Suspension Division that only handles suspended licenses.

Remember time is not on your side. With a suspended license, most often it will take up to two weeks to lock down how it was suspended. If you registered your car and paid with a check and the check bounced, they will suspend your license until the check is paid. How do I know? Because when I was interviewing with the Police Department to get a job as an officer, the Sergeant informed me that my license was suspended. I truly had no idea! The interview was on a Saturday, and you best believe that I was at the front door of the Department of Motor Vehicles the next business day to find out what happened, so I could get my license restored.

So, once you have determined why your license was suspended, get busy working some overtime. Call your mom and borrow some money so you can pay your fines. If it is a situation of an old case or a case in which you may need a lawyer to do an inquiry, don't get discouraged. Just stay focused. Take a day between 8 A.M. and 12 P.M. and call around to some lawyers and departments to get to the bottom of your suspension. If you are able to resolve the issues and get your license restored, the Department of Motor Vehicles will issue you a restoration notice. That is your temporary real license.

Most states require that you keep that restoration notice with you at all times when you are driving for up to one year.

That is because the information that is put in the Department of Motor Vehicles computer to remove the suspension status on your license is sometimes delayed. Thus, when you are pulled over a month or two later, the police computer shows that your license is still suspended and, minus that restoration notice, you will be dealt with as if it were still suspended.

So, save yourself the headache. I would suggest that you make several copies of the restoration notice. Make one and place in the glove compartment of your car. Make one and place in your court case portfolio file. If you have a lawyer representing you, give him/her a copy. Make a copy and keep in your house with your VIP papers. And make an extra copy to give to the court. Now don't be cheap. Make good copies. Your best bet is to go to Staples or Office Max and tell them to make you a color copy. Even though the document will be black and white, a color copy of a black and white is almost identical to the original. The goal here is to have a clear undisputable document.

- **A revoked license** – I suggest you get an attorney
- **A 300 series style license** (a license that was suspended before you even received your official license because the violations were received before the person actually had been issued a driver's license) – you may well need at least to consult with a lawyer, and you probably will have some considerable amount of fines to pay before they will even open your case.

■ **An international license** – You basically have to follow the same procedure as if you have no license. Since 9/11, many states have changed their requirements for application for a motor vehicle license. Pre-9/11, if you were visiting the United States and had a visa or passport, you could drive almost anywhere using your international license. If you were going to be in the United States on a work visa or student visa, you could use your international license or go to the local DMV and exchange it for a state license. Now, in 2009, if you have an international license in the United States and you are driving, the vast majority of police departments will deal with you as if you have no license.

I knew of a case in 2005, when a Moroccan friend of mine was pulled over in an East Coast state by the local police. At the time, he was driving with an international license, working legitimately in the United States, and he had a green card. The officers who stopped him called in an officer assigned to the terrorist unit. This officer, who was a Sergeant, had the patrol officers who conducted the motor vehicle stop seize the Moroccan's international driver's license. They took a copy of his green card and other identification and forwarded it to the immigration office of that state. All of that, for a failure to signal, a motor vehicle violation that was eventually overturned and, since he had a state license as well, the case was thrown out of court. However, given the full extent of the investigation to involve members of a special Terrorist Task Force, you can see why I strongly suggest that you have your documents in order!

Now that you have dealt with the license issue, which is often the most time-consuming part of resolving the case, you must move on to the next task. It is time to get insurance and this will be the start of the *money train*. Remember! The thing about owning a car in America is all about consumer finance. You buy something and you will have to continue to buy more things just to keep the first thing. Then, on top of that, you are mandated to buy the right to use it. And you have to spend the money because you need to use it, in this case a car, for a basic necessity to make more money in order to live.

> So can you avoid having car insurance? Yeah, in some situations.
>
> However, you certainly can't afford to do without it. It's too risky.

Fixing the Car Insurance

Car insurance is tricky. You may have some other dynamics that will determine how you may have to approach the whole car insurance piece. Motor vehicle insurance and motor vehicle registration go hand in hand. In most states, you must have proof of valid automobile insurance in order to register a motor vehicle. However, you do not need proof of registration in order to get insurance. However, even that may be based on your location within the United States.

In 1994, you could call one of the larger automobile insurance companies and give them all of your motor vehicle information over the phone. They would fax the temporary insurance cards to an insurance agent. You would then go into the insurance agent's office, show picture identification, sign for the cards, and sign a contract. Once you picked up the cards, your policy would be active and your coverage begins. If you knew exactly what company you would be getting insurance from, this entire procedure start to finish takes about eight hours or less. So, you can estimate that it will take about that long in 2009.

In fact, it is even easier to get insurance now than it was 10 years ago because of technology and competition from other insurance companies. You can call or even go online and fill out car insurance applications, pay online or over the phone with a credit card and the company will e-mail you or fax you the temporary insurance cards. From start to finish, this procedure can take less than 30 minutes, and your policy will begin. The key for you is that you must have a copy of the temporary insurance card in order to complete the motor vehicle registration. So writing down the policy number on a piece of paper or on the motor vehicle registration application will not be enough.

If by some chance you fall into one of the following categories, I suggest that you carefully follow these instructions. Remember that motor vehicle registration may vary slightly form state to state. So, check with your appropriate DMV for insurance guidelines.

Normally there are two categories you will fall into when it comes to the issue of motor vehicle insurance - owner and non-owner. If you:

- Are the owner, purchased a car and all you have is the title and bill of sale, you need to make sure that both have been signed over to you, so that you will be prepared to register the car. You also will need that proof for the insurance agency (the temporary insurance card).

- Are the owner and have had a previous car registration that expired, you need to determine if your insurance is valid. Do not assume! Call the insurance company and give them the policy number and ask them if the policy is active. If it is, tell them to send you the insurance declaration page to your policy. The insurance declaration page is the summary page. It contains all of the vital information necessary to prove that a policy has been officially set up. Though a police officer could care less about a declaration page, it will serve as a vital piece of information for your court case.

I would suggest that you make several copies. Place one in the glove compartment of your car. Place one in your court case portfolio file. If you have a lawyer representing you, give him/her a copy. Make a copy and keep it in your house with your VIP papers. And make an extra copy to give to the court. Don't be cheap. Make good copies. Your best bet is to go to Staples or Office Max and tell them to make a color copy. Even though the document will be black and white, a color copy of a black and white is almost identical to the original copy. The goal here is to have a clear, undisputable document to provide if needed.

■ Are not the owner of the car and were just using the car when you were stopped, depending on the laws of your state, you may not be responsible for insurance on a car you don't own. You can't insure a vehicle if you don't own it.

In a situation in which you are held liable or accountable for the insurance, you need to get the owner of the car to provide you with a valid insurance card. Make a clear copy of the card. And also have them get you a copy of the declaration page as well. I would suggest that you make several copies. Make one and place it in the glove compartment of the car. Make one and place it in your court case portfolio file. If you have a lawyer representing you, give him/her a copy. Make a copy and keep it in your house with your VIP papers. And make an extra copy to give to the court. Now don't be cheap. Make good copies. Your best bet is to go to Staples or Office Max and tell them to make a color copy. Even though the document will be black and white, a color copy of a black and white is almost identical to the original copy. Again, the goal here is to have a clear undisputable document.

Fixing the Car Registration

The final step in your mission to get your butt out of this motor vehicle nightmare is to get the car registered. First, make sure that you have a copy of the following before you even think about going to your local Department of Motor Vehicles office:

1. **At least two good pens for writing**
2. **Valid driver's license**
3. **Valid insurance card**
4. **Signed motor vehicle title**
5. **Bill of Sale, signed and dated**
6. **A checkbook or, preferably cash**
7. **The whole day to spend there**

This is not *play it cheap*! You need to be prepared, especially if you live far from the DMV or maybe have a tight schedule or live in an area where the DMV may only be open a few days a week. Also keep in mind that this is generally something that you cannot do on your lunch break and be back to work in time. So once you have gotten all of your documents in order, you will be ready. Now for some of you around the country you may run into a snag. Since 9/11, most states require that you have a valid driver's license before you can register a car. So, in the case of your license, if you don't have one by the time you are ready to get the car registered, just have someone else register it, like your mother, father or a relative who may live with you or live close to you. The issue for the court is not that you specifically have the car registered in your name; but that the car (which is a liability) is registered and insured (thus it is no longer a liability). Before you leave for the DMV, if you did not get your license renewed, reinstated or issued, be sure to bring one of the above-mentioned persons who has a valid license to register the car for you.

Now the glitch in doing this is that the person who registers the car must also have it insured in his/her name. In this case, I would suggest that you have your name added to the insurance policy as well. That way when you finally get your license issued, you could drive the car officially. Why? In some states, if you are not listed on the insurance policy, you can't drive the car. The other thing to remember is whoever's name the vehicle is registered in is considered the legal owner.

> **Whoever's name the vehicle is registered in is considered the legal owner.**

This is really important because you don't want to have your friend register your Lexus for you and then decide that he/she is going to go out of town without you. Or have your aunt register it, decides to let your cousin drive it, and he/she may be a licensed driver, but a poor driver. The bottom line is, in all situations, you would not have a say because you technically don't own the car!

If you fear filling out the form because it may seem to be confusing, just ask one of the attendants to help. You can also go to a used car dealership; they have many of the motor vehicle forms you will need, and they can help you fill them out. With all paperwork in order, the most important part to the registration is having the money. I would suggest that your first form of payment is cash. The last thing you want to do at this point is to write a bounced check to the DMV.

In some cases, if you write a bounced check you must pay a costly service fee. In other cases, if you write a bounced check it may be an immediate suspension of your driver's license, and in other cases, you may be issued an arrest warrant. So if you can, pay cash, money order or cashier's check, and make sure that you get a receipt and make several copies as I have instructed you to do for the previous documents.

Reviewing Your Case File

If you are diligent and persistent, you can have all of these documents together in a matter of five to ten business days. Now, I must be clear and say that it will cost you some money. You will have to buy car insurance, and the initial policy installment can average $150-$400. The insurance rates depend on where you live, your driving record, the type of car, and type of policy. I would assume you would get a basic liability policy. Often, you can pay the insurance company with a check. Some companies have such large accounts that your check won't clear for about two to three weeks. This is obviously very important if you are pressed for cash and time. The bottom line is that the court wants to know if the car has valid insurance, not that you're trying to beat the check you wrote to the bank next Friday.

The next cost is the license renewal, reinstatement or whatever it takes to make it valid. The cost could be from zero to infinity based on your individual situation. And there is the cost of your registration, which again will depend on the make, year and model of your vehicle, the town you reside in and the length of time you must register it. In some states you may only be required to register it for six months and in others, you may have to register it for a minimum of two years. So, the minimum amount normally can run from $75 to $250. Don't get crazy and try and register your car with vanity plates (specialized plates with your name on it, like "LUCKY-1"). Why? The registration fees on these plates are extremely high and can cost up to $400 in some cases. Just get a basic "made in the state prison using your tax dollars" license plate. Why? The judge will not be impressed because you came back to court with a custom registration plate or marker plate.

The next piece to this is to review your case file. Get out all of the documents that you have been keeping. In one folder, keep all of your original papers. That is your file. You don't give your original file to anyone. Even after the court case is over, you should keep your original file at home with your very important papers forever. I still have a restoration notice from 1991 filed in my papers at home. Why? Because, you never know when you may need them again. You should create additional folders for the court prosecutor, the judge, your lawyer (give him two in case you need one), and one extra. Make sure each folder has the same information. Label the folders "Attorney So-and-So," "Judge," "Prosecutor." Label the extra one "File." Now you are almost ready.

Preparing for Court

Let me be crystal clear and say that the key to getting your case nolled or dismissed does not rest solely on you taking care of the required documents, but also on your appearance. In the book *Black Robes, White Justice*, author Bruce Wright, a Black judge, shares his views on the issues within the American criminal court system. He describes the position of a Black defendant in a courtroom as being one in which the odds are often stacked against him. Wright cites Pascal's Theory of Self Determination as the basis of the decisions of a non-Black, -Latino, or -Hispanic judge. I view it as socioeconomic cognitive dissonance, which occurs when the judge relates better to a defendant who is of the judge's race, ethnicity, economic status and level of education. In cases in which the defendant fits these criteria, the judge is more likely to provide options to resolving the case that would cause the least social and economic hardship on the defendant.

If you don't fall into these qualifications, you will probably be a part of what I call the "meat wagon." You will then be on your way to the slaughterhouse for processing, probation, fines, jail time, or hard time. And, for every category you fail, you increase your chances for punishment and decrease your options for resolution. It's like a credit report on your character. So, you are probably asking yourself, "How can I then have a chance?"

Give yourself a chance!

Any day, you can walk down to the local courthouse and see the biggest show in town. There you will see a 50 Cent look-a-like pleading guilty to a felony case. You will most likely see a J-Lo look-a-like dressed  in a Toni Braxton skirt talking about how she wants her baby's daddy locked up!

You have to understand that, as I said in the previous lessons, you will be dealing with people within the criminal justice system who are human beings. They have faults and some of them will be stereotyping the population of people with whom they work. And, as in most cases of stereotyping, they don't deal with you based on what YOU know; they deal with you based on what THEY know.

So, if you come to court dressed like a thug. The chances are you're...

Right, you're a drug dealer, a gang member, or a person who carries illegal guns.

If you come to court with your chest showing down to your nipple pads, your pants tight and your thong visible, then chances are you're...

Right, you're a stripper who loves to have sex and worries more about how you look than how you act

So, before you go back to court, get it together!

The following is a **list of items you will need to successfully defeat any negative images about** you as a young Black, Latino/Hispanic male:

- Wear a grey or dark-colored suit and tie. Go to Goodwill. (They have nice suits for $12 that are worth $120, and they have silk ties for $1 that are worth $25).
- Wear a clean white shirt. Make sure it's ironed. Bring it to the cleaners if possible and tell them to use medium starch (that will cost you $2).

■ Wear clean socks, preferably black or dark blue.

Now, if for some reason if you cannot get your hands on a suit, at least wear a collared shirt, a tie, and a pair of dark colored slacks. I suggest a paisley tie, white shirt, and black pants.

■ Wear a black leather dress pant belt (without a nameplate).

■ Wear black or darker colored dress shoes.

■ Do not wear sneakers, boots or "Tims."

■ Do not wear earrings (for men only).

■ Do not wear piercing rings (nose, eyebrow, chin, lip).

■ Do not wear sunglasses in the courthouse at any time.

■ Do not wear gold fronts (gold teeth inserts).

■ Do not wear jewelry (gold chains, "bling" watches).

■ Do not wear a baseball, knit hat, or "fitted hat"

■ Do not wear gloves in the courthouse.

■ Do not wear a football or baseball jacket.

■ Do not wear a flight jacket.

Make sure you get a new haircut. I'm not saying cut off your dreads. Relax! I'm just saying at least get an edge up, wash your hair and make it look neat. The more conservative your hair style, the better. I know of a court case in which a white cop was on trial for manslaughter for a police-related shooting involving an unarmed Jamaican male. When he was tried the first time, he wore a bald-headed hairstyle. He lost the case. His lawyer suggested to him to grow some hair on his head. I spoke with his attorney and asked him why he told the cop to grow hair. He told me that since the cop was a white male, having a shaved head made him look too much like a "skin head," and he believed that perception played into the jury's judgment.

The attorney told me that, by having his client grow hair, it brought his appearance back into the perception of the American mainstream. So, listen to me. Get a haircut! It will only cost you about $20 and could save you hundreds of dollars in fines and court fees.

Moving on, don't wear any cologne. Just because it smells good to you, does not mean it smells good to everyone else. And, in a closed area where you may be with a prosecutor or judge, if they have allergies and you irritate their condition, you ain't helpin' your cause. However, do wear deodorant. Wear a lot of deodorant because you will probably be nervous. Also, as a note if you can, buy some non-scented deodorant. Make sure your lips aren't chapped. Cut your fingernails. Make sure they are clean. You may not realize that men with long nails have long been associated with illegal drug lifestyles and other criminal activity. So, you may think it's cute and fly; again, you ain't helpin'. Put on some lotion. Don't go in the courtroom with your hands looking like you were punching a bag of flour.

And, finally, take a good look in the mirror. If you were successful in following my instructions, when you go to court, other people should mistake you for a lawyer or some other court staff. You get it. So what is the science behind this? Well, if someone reminded you of someone you cared about, would you hurt that person or would you reason with them about why they got into that predicament (an arrest)? Most likely, you would excuse them for making the mistake. It was because of something lacking in their environment. Or, you would give them the benefit of the doubt. So now, you get it!

Once you have gotten your dress together and you have your case file, just make sure you go to court on the scheduled date. Or, maybe in your case, the rescheduled date. BE ON TIME! In fact, get there 30 minutes beforehand and see if you can speak with the prosecutor handling your case. You may be able to settle it without even being required to appear before the judge. Remember, the judge is a busy person and has tons of nothing to do. So, the judge prefers to have as much free time as possible. And the prosecutor's job is to sift through all of the labor-intensive paperwork and "make it plain" for the judge. The prosecutor really doesn't have time for your case. Motor vehicle cases often tie up valuable court time. So, the sooner they can resolve your case, the happier they are.

And, after all that hard work, the dress, the documents, the shopping, watching Judge Joe Brown, practicing in the mirror, sweating, worrying and borrowing money, you arrive at court. Then you show the prosecutor all of your paperwork and he tells you,

"Ok, good! Just see the clerk and pay a $100 court fee, and you'll be all set."

In most cases, you will be speechless, thinking that you were going to go to jail. Then you will realize, like I said in the previous lesson, it's business; it's always about business. So, you paid $100 for five minutes of the court's time. Actually, you spent five minutes with the State Prosecutor, who is employed by the State and paid with your tax dollars, and all the money you spent dealing with car registration and licenses again went to the State. It is about business. So, don't forget to bring lots of money to court.

Lesson 2: Knowledge is Power

Ten Years of Contemporary Policing

Use of Force

(EXCERPTS TAKEN FROM U.S. DEPARTMENT OF JUSTICE OFFICE OF COMMUNITY ORIENTED POLICING SERVICES WEBSITE)

Every day, law enforcement officers face danger while carrying out their responsibilities. When dealing with a dangerous—or unpredictable—situation, police officers usually have very little time to assess it and determine the proper response. Here, good training can enable the officer to react properly to the threat or possible

27

threat and respond with the appropriate tactics to address the situation, possibly including some level of force, *if necessary*, given the circumstances.

The U.S. Commission on Civil Rights has stated that "...in diffusing situations, apprehending alleged criminals, and protecting themselves and others, officers are legally entitled to use appropriate means, including force." In dozens of studies of police use of force there is no single, accepted definition among the researchers, analysts, or the police. The International Association of Chiefs of Police (IACP) in its study, *Police Use of Force in America 2001*, defined use of force as "The amount of effort required by police to compel compliance by an unwilling subject." The IACP also identified five components of force: physical, chemical, electronic, impact, and firearm.

To some people, though, the mere presence of a police officer can be intimidating and seen as use of force.

The Bureau of Justice Statistics (BJS) in *Data Collection on Police Use of Force*, states that "...the legal test of excessive force...is whether the **police officer *reasonably* believed that such force was *necessary*** to accomplish a legitimate police purpose..." However, there are no universally accepted definitions of **"reasonable" and "necessary" because the terms are subjective.** A court in one jurisdiction may define "reasonable" or "necessary" differently than a court in a second jurisdiction. More to the point is an understanding of the "improper" use of force, which can be divided into two categories: "unnecessary" and "excessive." The unnecessary use of force would be the application of force where there is no justification for its use, while an excessive use of force would be the application of more force than required where use of force is necessary.

Contacts between Police and the Public, a 1999 BJS report, estimated that less than half of one percent of an estimated 44 million people who had face-to-face contact with a police officer were threatened with or actually experienced force. Other studies report similar statistics. It is these few situations, however, that attract public attention. Robert K. Olsen, former Minneapolis Police Chief and Past President, Police Executive Research Forum (PERF), early in 2004 called the use of force "the single most volatile issue facing police departments." He noted that "just one use of force incident can dramatically alter the stability of a police department and its relationship with a community."

Police department policies can have a significant impact on how force is used in street-level encounters, says a 2003 study by the Community Relations Services of the U.S. Department of Justice, *Principles of Good Policing: Avoiding Violence Between Police and Citizens.* And, the BJS Data Collection report mentioned above stresses the need for police executives to improve training of recruits and police officers on the use of force and the techniques for minimizing its application.

Between 1996 and 2007, the tri-state area (the East Coast states of Connecticut, New York, and New Jersey) was inundated with incidents between police and the public that were controversial cases of alleged police brutality, which was an understatement in most cases. On April 14, 1997, in New Haven Connecticut, what would start out as routine police patrol of a minor traffic complaint ended in a police chase (two white East Haven cops) with the unarmed 21-year-old Black male, **Malik Jones** fatally shot. This was the introduction to what was yet to come in the tri-state area. On August 9, 1997, in East Flatbush New York City, a group of white cops sexually assaulted a Haitian male (again, a young Black male). **Abner Louima**, who was arrested at "Club Rendez-Vous," a popular nightclub in East Flatbush, for charges that could have been addressed by issuing him a misdemeanor summons ticket and giving him a Promise to Appear in court. The arresting officers beat Louima with their fists, nightsticks, and hand-held police radios on the ride to the station.

On arriving at the station house, he was strip-searched and put in a holding cell. The beating continued later, culminating with Louima being raped in a bathroom at the 70th Precinct station house in Brooklyn. Officer Justin Volpe kicked Louima in the testicles, then, while Louima's hands were cuffed behind his back, he first grabbed onto and squeezed his testicles and then sodomized him with a plunger, causing severe internal damage to his colon and bladder that required several operations to repair. Volpe then walked through the precinct holding the bloody, excrement-stained instrument in his hand, indicating that he had "broke a man down."

Louima's teeth were also badly damaged in the attack by having the broomstick jammed into his mouth. The day after the incident, Louima was transferred to the Coney Island Hospital emergency room. Escorting officers explained away his serious injuries being a result of "abnormal homosexual activities." An emergency room nurse, Magalie Laurent, suspecting the nature of Louima's extreme injuries were not the result of gay sex, notified Louima's family and the Police Department's Internal Affairs Bureau of the likelihood of sexual assault and battery. Louima was hospitalized for two months after the incident.

Again in New Milford Connecticut, on December 29, 1998, **Franklyn Reid** a 27-year-old unarmed Jamaican male fleeing from the police in a foot chase was fatally **shot in the back** while laying on his stomach at gunpoint by a white cop. The officer claimed that he shot the subject in the back after the subject attempted to reach for a weapon. At trial, evidence was presented that showed Officer Scott Smith's footprint on the Reid's back.

In New York City on February 4, 1999, America would see unchanged law enforcement and the epitome of racial profiling at its finest. A group of white cops (dressed in plain clothes) shot unarmed Muslim male from Guinea, **Aqhmed Amadu Diallo**, while he stood in the foyer of his apartment building getting his keys or wallet from his pocket. The four cops shot at him a horrific 41 times and the Muslim male was struck 19 times by police gunfire. What started out with a "subject fitting the description" ended in a positive identification of what I call "The State of America's outlook on Black males."

Then on April 13, 1999 (only four months following the fatal shooting in Connecticut of December 29, 1998), a white police officer in Hartford Connecticut's capital city gunned down a fleeing youth suspected in a robbery. The youth was 14-year-old **Aquan Salmon**, a young Black male from an inner city area of town. Evidence presented showed that the youth had purchased a cigarette lighter that resembled a handgun; there was never any mention that the youth was in possession of it at the time of the shooting. On March 16, 2000, in midtown Manhattan, New York again picked up the baton, when another undercover operation gone bad resulted in the fatal shooting of unarmed 26-year-old **Patrick Dorismond**, a Black male off-duty security guard who was suspected of having or wanting a small amount of drugs. In this incident, the twist was that the cop was Hispanic and the shooting happened in an upscale area rather than in the inner city. Once again, the suspect was unarmed. Moreover, as in the previously mentioned NYPD shooting, the suspect was mistaken for someone else and was innocent. Then, early morning on November 25, 2008, undercover crime unit officers who fired 50 shots gunned down **Sean Bell** a 23-year-old unarmed Black male coming from his bachelor party. One of the officers was reported as having fired 31 bullets, causing him to reload two times. Damn!

Sounds like a war? This is only a snapshot of some of the actions and results of actions that have involved police and the public since 1996 in the tri-state area. The irony is, in all of the incidents that I have highlighted, all of the subjects killed were unarmed and no weapons were recovered at the scene. Also, they were all Black males. So we could put it to a test. How would you categorize these events?

A) *Racism in law enforcement*

B) *Racial police departments*

C) *Racial profiling*

D) *Socially-imbedded stereotypes*

E) *Ignorance about Blacks as well other cultures and groups*

It is tough to pick just one, but it is even more serious to members of the Black and Latino/Hispanic community when it seems that they are the only ones singled out.

Some so-called Black and Latino/Hispanic leaders have considered these events to be an epidemic within the Black community. However, I beg to differ because an epidemic is unpredictable and often there at least a vague hope for a cure. These events are the result of *piss poor policing*, and the culture of law enforcement nationwide ignorance about Blacks, Latinos and other People of Color. Education plays a major role in this change, along with new laws that deter this type of behavior. Public outcries on these issues only seem to serve as a controlled arena for increasing church congregations and as platforms for political leaders to jumpstart their campaigns.

Remember that in February of 1999, regarding the Aqhmed Amadu Diallo shooting in New York City, President Bill Clinton made public his discontent with the shooting of 41 bullets at an unarmed man. And yet, not only were the cops found **not guilty** by the State, but also they were cleared federally in 2001. To further put it in the face of the Black community, the NYPD or Mayor Julliani did not even find the officers in violation of department policy and/or procedures. This showed that not even the opinion of the President of the United States of America could influence

change when it comes to the racial issues engraved in America's law
enforcement agencies.

The affect that these events had on community and police
relations in the inner city as well as in the suburbs has been
devastating. After a while, white folks finally realized that this
was obviously a serious problem. Though it did not involve
them directly, it involved them indirectly because 99.9% of the
cops who were pulling the trigger were white. It is my theory
that the actions of these officers brought a blemish to the image
of White male professionals and other white folks, too. They
began to react as many Blacks have for years. They wanted to
let the rest of America see that they were not like that and that
these few officers did not represent the mentality and actions for
all of white America. They did not want these incidents to
portray a negative view about white people. Moreover,
government officials could not afford to have whites in authority
stereotyped as malicious, reckless, untrustworthy and
incompetent. It would become clear that what few ties remained
between Black and White America after the O.J. Simpson trial
had now become severely strained.

In addition to that, many hate crimes would occur
throughout the U.S., such as the brutal dragging of a Black
male in Jasper, Texas by a group of white males who belonged
to one of the many white supremacist groups. This would serve

as one of those terrible events that would linger in the minds of most Black Americans. National race relations in the U.S. would resemble more of a boiling pot than a melting pot.

Again, there would be a national focus on an issue that has existed in the United States since before the Emancipation Proclamation: *Black people and White police.* More considerable incidents occurred, which would give birth to the phase "DWB" (Driving While Black). It became the upscale version of racial profiling; a phrase that was coined only after white officers had victimized many bourgeois Blacks. Some police departments found this to be absurd but, as you will later find in reading this book, the truth was revealed. New Jersey would become one of the focal points because, while traveling New Jersey's highways, many minorities had complained about being pulled over based only on their race. Initially, officials within the New Jersey State Police vehemently denied this. Then, two white New Jersey State Troopers fired 11 shots at a van they had stopped on the New Jersey Turnpike. The vehicle contained four young Black/Hispanic males; three of the four occupants suffered gunshot wounds. None of them were armed. No weapons or drugs were ever recovered. After that, the Black community in the tri-state area was in an uproar and, as usual, no one wanted to hear anything.

The Black community was no longer interested in talk. It was time for the truth.

So in 1998, Colonel Carl Williams, Superintendent of the State Police since 1994, who was also known as "The Truth," would go on record with the public to confirm what all of Black America had known and felt all along. In an interview with *The Star-Ledger,* he stated that the State Police never would or never should use racial profiling when determining who gets pulled over on New Jersey's highways. However, he went on to state that he would be truthful in saying that there was racial profiling to drug crimes.

He gave the following examples: Jamaicans (Blacks) control the heroin market, white bikers control the trade in methamphetamines, and when it comes to the "big problems" such as cocaine and marijuana, "it is most likely a minority group (Blacks and Hispanics) that's involved with that."

After Colonel Williams told the truth and the newspapers printed the statement, New Jersey Governor Christie Whitman immediately hooked him up with a big fat pink slip. About time!

The irony to Williams' theory is simple. Almost all of the groups mentioned who would be operating a motor vehicle, would be Black or Hispanic and thus there would be no need to pull over white people unless they were on a bike or riding a motorcycle.

The bottom line is that there are obvious imperfections in policing. Why? Because police officers are humans and, like all humans, they have imperfections. However, this should not be an excuse, because the public holds an officer to a higher standard and entrust them with their safety. The next Lesson Street Lawyer, will talk about what you need to do when you are dealing with the police, when you are talking to the police and when you are interacting with the police. Sometimes it will often come down to one simple old phrase, "You get what you give!"

> **The truth is real, it's scary, and it always returns to reveal itself.**

Lesson 3: Street Lawyer

Using Proper Etiquette When You are Speaking to Police

The number one complaint that citizens file against police officers is for verbal abuse. In most cases, the incident occurred during the course of a motor vehicle stop. Often, the citizen reports that he was pulled over "for no reason," and the officer began to yell at him "for no reason" and then began to harass and insult him "for no reason." The irony is that most of these complaints are filed after a citizen has been arrested during that motor vehicle stop. And, when the Internal Affairs Division begins to investigate the case, the investigator finds that, in most cases, the citizen became loud and rowdy with the officer, which led to the officer arresting the citizen for disorderly conduct or interfering with a police investigation.

In all cases like this, the charges are classified as a misdemeanor and could have been avoided if the citizen had utilized one basic but valuable tool, courtesy. Yes, believe it or not, it is often a person's ego that gets him a free ride to detention. Historically, most circumstances that have involved conflict between police and young African American and Latino/Hispanic males have been the result of a "failure to communicate" by all parties. What you need to know is if the police come up short on communication skills, it will not result in the officer going to jail. You will be the one to pay the price! So pay close attention! Has this happened to you?

Monster Stop

True Story: *It was the late summer of 1990, when my good friend Kazz and I were traveling from Carrollton, Georgia, to Connecticut. I was operating a 1986 Mercury Topaz that was registered in my father's name (we had the same last name) and the car was registered and insured in Connecticut. I had a Georgia state driver's license, as I was a college student in Georgia at the time. My car was in good condition and had no tinted windows. We were on*

Interstate 95 traveling north through Bellaire, Maryland, when we observed an unmarked state trooper patrol car behind us.

The car was in the middle lane at the time, so I immediately signaled right and pulled over to the emergency lane. The traffic conditions were very heavy, and the car was loaded up with luggage so the entire back seat was filled up to the windows. Kazz was seated in the front passenger seat.

When I pulled over to the side and stopped the car, the trooper got out of his car and approached us on the passenger side window. He was a white officer who stood about six feet tall. Kazz rolled down the window and the officer slightly leaned toward the car. He asked the usual, "Where are y'all comin' from? What's your name? Where yah live?" I told him we both lived in Georgia and that my car was registered in Connecticut because my father let me use it while I was at school. I then told him that my license was in a bag in the back seat. He stated that my car was not registered because I lived in Georgia, but I explained to him that the car was not really mine. However, I knew that there was more to the stop than my registration.

Since I used my "fool proof plan" (when stopped by police be very polite, articulate and alert), he seemed to have picked up on it and directed his attention to my friend Kazz (the front seat passenger). He asked Kazz for his license and Kazz told him that he did not need his license because he was not driving. At that point, the trooper got angry and leaned into the car and had an exchange of words with Kazz. I do not recall exactly what was said, but the conversation ended with the officer ordering us from the vehicle in a hostile fashion. He told Kazz to step out of the car, but the officer was leaning on the car door, which prevented Kazz from opening it. Again the officer told Kazz to get out of the car, and Kazz told him that he would when the officer moved off of the car door. I knew then we were in for an event. Once we were outside of the car, we were frisked and the officer told Kazz to stand by the rail on the side of the road. He followed and watched me while I got my license from the car. When I opened my suitcase, the officer saw large clear freezer bags that contained a green leafy substance. What he did not know was that it was not drugs. I immediately told him that it was herbal tea and invited him to smell it. He did so and that seemed to break the tension. I was relieved because I knew that the police don't play in the South, and I considered Maryland to be definitely "Mississippi Burning" territory.

Despite my anxieties, things were looking up for us. The officer let both of us sit on the guardrail while he went back into his car to continue the investigation. Suddenly, a marked state trooper car pulled up and out jumped a Black cop who stood about six feet tall and had a slender build. He looked like Damon Wayans, the actor/comedian. However, he acted like the Black cop we all dreaded to encounter. He walked up to us, and we said "hello." He *immediately told us to get on the ground. We asked where? Only the emergency lane was available, and we could not believe that he wanted us to get on that dirty ground. We already had been frisked. The wind was blowing very hard, and the sandy dust and dirt were swirling around. But, yes, he did want us to get face down on the ground. Now I was mad, and I knew that this was a bunch of nonsense. Kazz and I both knew that this was a classic case of "showing off for the white man." A short time later, after they had searched the car and found nothing, we were able to get up. Our clothes were covered with dirt and dust. We each had one side of our face covered with dirt. The white officer approached us and looked at us as though he was embarrassed by the actions of the Black trooper. He gave me a warning ticket for speeding and a ticket for having a suspended license; I later made a trip to Maryland to have it thrown out of court after paying a bogus $100.00 court fee.*

The attitude of the white officer at the end of the stop was completely opposite from the Black officer. This was a prime example that the color of the officer who stops you is not important. What is important is that the officer has compassion and is not overbearing during the stop. The Black officer who gave us a lecture about drugs and guns never said a word after we got up. He stayed off to the side as though we had the plague. He would later remind me of the Black cop who was in the John Singleton's 1992 movie, *"Boys N the Hood."*

> **The color of the officer who stops you is not important. What is important is that the officer has compassion and is not overbearing during the stop.**

That event was typical of most motor vehicle stops. Normally the officer either starts off nice or the officer is out to get you from the start. You must remember to use what I call the "fool proof plan" at all times, and do nothing verbally and/or physically to provoke the officer. Most officers prefer to have the operator and occupants remain in the car, so if you're being told to step out of the car, either you have set off flags, alerted the officer that something is suspicious or he is already suspicious of you. Kazz is a good example of why simple motor vehicle stops can lead to arrest. Remember, criminal law is not written in favor of the citizens and, in some cases, exercising freedom of speech during a motor vehicle stop can lead to a misdemeanor arrest for interfering with a police investigation, obstruction of justice or the appropriate criminal term depending on what state you are in at the time.

These types of police and community engagements with the inner city residents and members of the Black and Hispanic community have been on going challenges. They are events that have been continuously covered by the *"Nightly News," "60 Minutes,"* Time Warner, local newspapers, and *USA Today.* It would appear that the media spends the bulk of their time portraying people of color in America as the usual menace to society, which only further gives validity to various unofficial law enforcement techniques and tactics that add fuel to the fire for the historically poor relationship between police and the community.

On March 3, 1991 the *truth* would again surface in the world of in-just-us in America. A Black male motorist in Los Angeles, California refused to stop his vehicle for Los Angeles police officers. They pursued him in what they described as a high-speed chase. After the Black male was finally stopped, several officers performed what defense attorneys would later argue was "normal police procedure." That normal procedure resulted in the motorist being shot with a high voltage stun gun and several officers *slave beat* him at will using their new state-of-the-art police batons called PR-24 (Personal Restraint Batons). The PR-24 measures approximately 26 inches and is made of aircraft aluminum steel; a PR-24 cannot break or bend. What was amazing was not how many times the officers hit him, but that they repeatedly beat him even after he had submitted and was on the ground displaying very little movement. Fortunately, the entire incident was captured on a home video camera by the smartest person in America. Even after seeing the video again and again, it is hard to believe that there are people in America with so much anger and hatred towards Blacks that they would consciously perform such an act.

What is even more frightening is that often these people were officers. More disturbing is that they were in the company of a supervisor who condoned the officers' behavior. Unlike the ol' Southern stories, this one happened on the West Coast, in a so-called liberal city. The motorist, Rodney King, did not have a weapon at the time of the stop, and he had not committed a violent or major crime. However, he was served his punishment premature to his court date.

These officers again widened the color gap between the relationship of Blacks, Latino/Hispanics and whites in America. It reminded me about an incident in which my friend and I were stopped for carrying a BB-gun, what happened to him when he ran from the police, and what they did to him when he was caught.

Many Blacks in America called it a "wake up call" (as depicted in this drawing "King Me") and demanded immediate justice. They began staging public rallies, producing tee shirts, buttons and

KING ME

flyers, making public speeches, and participating in radio programs and BET (Black Entertainment Television) talk shows. On the other hand, many bourgeois Negroes who W.E.B. Du Bois described as the "talented tenth" (the cream of the crop of the Black community) referred to the incident as a "tragedy for all involved." Sounds familiar? This was the classic non-controversial response among those in Black America (the "house Negroes" As Malcolm X called them), who have bought into the ideas of the Euro-American tradition. They are enchanted with what we know as the American Dream, a strong possibility for the so-called middle class non-minorities. It is a maze of deception for all others, filled with politically correct excuses for the injustices. The ones who have given me inspiration to produce this book. Ok, I got a little carried away. But, the bottom line is that many in the Black community punk out on real issues facing the quality of life for young Black males.

Unfortunately for America, there was no response that could calm the tensions that amassed as a result of the Rodney King beating. For the first time in the history of the U.S.A., a Black person who was subjected to police misconduct/brutality was viewed as a victim, and that was paramount. He was not just seen as a victim by members of the Black community, but by members of all types of cultural and ethnic groups in America who had suffered similar episodes at the hands of law enforcement personnel. The officers were tried for police misconduct, found not guilty by an all-white jury and released. That sparked a national chain reaction of riots not seen in America since the post-Civil Rights movement in the early 1970s. The riots in Los Angeles alone would call for temporary martial law. Branches of the armed forces were brought into the city to control the social anarchy. The damages that resulted from the rioting cost the city of Los Angeles billions of dollars. I'm sure if the Los Angeles Police Chief could have turned back the clock he would have just fired them.

Effects were felt as far as New England. In New Haven, Connecticut, a small ice cream store that had operated in a suburban area adjacent to some housing projects was torched and defaced with Rodney King slogans. It would seem as though, over the next 16-month period, America's social infrastructure had reverted to the dark days of the 1950s and 1960s, as a result of the actions of a handful of police officers. Once again, the old and new generations of Blacks from that era of Ol' Southern oral tradition would introduce the idea that had lingered in the Black community for decades – the need for Black police in Black neighborhoods.

Unlike those who came before them, this new generation of urban Blacks was now running off of the furious reaction, energy, solidarity, and personal victimization of the Rodney King beating. They did not want dialogue. They wanted justice to be put into action. They demanded that Black police officers be put into the inner city communities to prevent future incidents like the Rodney King beating. They were no longer asking; they were demanding. Mad, upset, disappointed and scared, they had finally had enough. I knew many Black males, myself included, who were scared to drive, especially in suburban white towns. My colleagues, behavioral psychologists, were white males at an agency where I was working during the time of the King beating. They asked, "Why didn't he just stop?" I described it to them as a condition I termed as *Black anxiety*.

Black anxiety occurs when a vast majority of your mental thoughts are dedicated to worrying about what will happen when you encounter the police. Do you fit the description of someone else they are looking for in connection with a crime? Will a good officer or a "donut eating cop" a.k.a "rogue cop" stop you? If you have ever driven a car without a valid driver's license (such as a suspended license) or improper registration or no insurance, you knew you would get arrested or ticketed if you got stopped by the police.

Now remember how you felt when you suddenly passed a patrol car? Remember that feeling you had upon seeing the police car? And remember that feeling you had after you passed it? The hot flash, nervous actions, and the mental blackouts that were so profound that you forgot where you were supposed to be going – that's Black anxiety!

I know because I am writing from personal experience. Those are the same feelings experienced on a day-to-day basis by the vast majority of Black men, Black women, Latino men, Latino women, Hispanic men, Hispanic women and other minority cultures and sub-cultures living in America. I am confident that members of other cultural and ethnic groups also share this dilemma.

Unfortunately, almost every young Black and or Latino/Hispanic male has experienced Black Anxiety or will experience it before age 16, because of the past and present political inaction, social injustice and the maltreatment of various minority groups by law enforcement officers nationwide. As a result of the King beating and this so-called new awareness of the unjust treatment of Blacks by the police, more police misconduct incidents have been highlighted and reported. The media made it a priority-reporting topic, rap artists wrote about it in their songs, and so-called Black leaders spoke out against it. Even more phenomenal was that the courts were inundated with lawsuits that were filed against the local and state law enforcement departments. The cases almost always involved some type of police misconduct, which was dominated by reports of police brutality.

In the wake of the verdict in the Rodney King beating, it appeared as though Blacks had regained their second wind in pursuit of the mysterious goal long yearned for by those who came before them. The next two and half years would be filled with heavy reconciliatory dialogue. This was a frantic attempt by the powers-that-be to stabilize the still growing tension among minorities and other sympathizers in American inner cities. Most Blacks in America still had a bad taste in their mouths for white officials. Overall, the media highlighted programs and dialogues initiated by the bourgeoisie Negroes. They were made up of a collection of ministers, masons, public officials, political leaders and professionals who acted as the delivery boys to the Blacks in the urban cities. The bulk of the action for change would come from those who did not have a hidden agenda – the victims, the grassroots, and the day-to-day citizens in Black America.

Citizens of the Black community would have to wait until the mid 1990s before they would see a significant number of Black officers working in their community. These were true law enforcement officers, not just officers working under the premise that "White *fokes* have allowed us to work here at *dis* police department and *wees* should just shut up and *bees* grateful."

But, still not enough progress was being made. Events like the 1995 O. J. Simpson trial, which exposed the racist detective Marc Fuhrman, would again find its way into the present day lives of Black people in America. During that period of time, social and political awareness among Blacks was on the rise. The grassroots community groups had begun to form as a product of the social, political, and economic injustice that Blacks in America faced. The members of these groups were ordinary citizens from both the inner city and suburban side of the city who felt that the state and local officials were not interested in changing or addressing serious issues facing the people of the Black community. Talking and listening is just a small part of how change can occur. The main ingredient is education, knowledge, and action.

This reminds me of an incident that occurred in 1996 when I had just finished the police academy. I was now one of *them*, a police officer. Off-duty, though, I did not look like a cop. I still dressed very plainly and wore construction work-type apparel, and on occasion I wore African cultural clothing. The number one factor that would make me a suspect was my car. My car did not look like a car that a police officer drove. I had an 80s model Honda Civic 4-door. It was a little beat up, and the paint was very dull.

Nevertheless it was my car, and the closest thing I had to the automobile side of the American Dream.

The Cop Magnet

True Story: *It was the fall of 1996 and I had just finished the Police Academy. I was clean cut, physically fit, and of course proud to be an American and most of all to be a police officer in America. It was about 1:00 P.M. on a warm Sunday afternoon. It was sunny and the sky was clear and blue. You could say it was a perfect fall day. I had packed my family (my wife, my three-year-old son, and my one-year-old son) inside of the 1986 Honda Civic.*

We drove to a suburban town that had an upper middle class shopping center. The shopping center was located in a shopping plaza along with stores such as Home Depot and Sports Authority. The irony was that these stores were frequented predominately by Black and Hispanic people from outside of the town. I dropped my wife off at the grocery store, a discount store that is always crowded with customers. I then parked in the lot and remained in the car with my three-year-old old son. After about 30-40 minutes, I saw my wife emerging from the store with a cart full of groceries and my one-year-old son. I then pulled my car into the fire lane at the front of the store and left the car running so I could load the groceries into the car.

As I pulled up, I had observed a marked police cruiser passing me on the left. I could see him glaring at the car and at me as he passed. (At this point, my wife was not near the car). I knew from my limited training as a new cop that he was about to pull me over. I also knew from my vast experience as a Black male in America that he definitely would pull me over before I could get out of the car. And believe it or not, once he had passed me, I could see the cruiser making a U-turn and coming up to the rear of my car. Now understand the setting:

- *suburban shopping center*
- *sunny afternoon*
- *heavily saturated with shoppers.*
- *two cars parked in the fire lane in front of me.*

As the cruiser came towards the rear of my car, my wife and one-year-old son were approaching the car with the cart full of groceries. I had been down this road before, so I got out of the car before the cop did. AND I DON'T RECOMMEND THAT ANYONE DO THAT. One reason I got out of the car before him was to see how skilled he was with his tactics because a skilled officer never allows the occupant to get out of the car first. The other reason was because I was a police officer and knew the "rules to the game" that had been perpetrated against me and many others like me for so many years. I was torn between being a "New kind of Negro" and giving him a class on the rights that I had as a "complete citizen." So what I did was exit my car once his cruiser had stopped, and went to the rear passenger door on the driver's side where my one-year-old son was sitting. (It should be noted that he never used his emergency lights or siren, or any other signal that indicated to me that I was being stopped).) In the back window of my car was a department-issued traffic vest and I had placed it so that the officer would see it before he pulled me over.

Well, it did not work, because he pulled his cruiser so close to my car that I could not even walk around to the other side (Again, a very poor traffic stop tactic). I knew then I was dealing with a cop with his own agenda. Out of the car came a 6' 5" tall, White male cop. He appeared to be a Lieutenant or Sergeant and was about 50 years old. He walked right up to me and said, "Hi, I noticed that your emissions sticker has expired. I wonder if you could show me the paperwork for your car?"

Of course, I knew this was all "probable cause foolishness." This was the same foolishness that caused many other Black and Latino/Hispanic males to get locked up and fined. After he finished talking, I was torn between insult and laughter. It was amazing to have heard of it and to have seen it on television, but now I was having firsthand contact. I then took control of the situation. I pulled out my wallet, which displayed my driver's license and my shiny two-week-old badge. As I opened my wallet the sun reflected off of my badge so brightly that the glare went into the eyes of the Lieutenant. He then jerked his head back as if he had seen a ghost. I said, "Here is my license and registration" and handed them to him.

He said "Oh! You're with the unit?" This was a signal that indicated to me that he knew that I really had known why he had stopped me.

"Yes, I am," I replied very politely as I was very polite from the onset of the stop despite my frustrations. He then asked me how long I had been on. "About six months," I replied. The six months included my time at the academy.

"So you must know my friend, Sergeant Such-and-such?"

"Yes. As a matter of fact, he was my Field Training Officer Supervisor," I replied.

"Yeah, we go back a long way to the Interstate Detective Unit. He's an awesome guy!" he said.

The sergeant he was referring to was Puerto Rican. The Unit he was referring to was a statewide unit that pooled officers together from throughout the state into one unit. This is often known as a statewide task force.

"Yes, he is. Do you want my papers," I asked.
"Nawh, kid. You're all set. Be safe and take care."

Now I was pissed that, out of three cars doing the same thing in the same place, I was the only one selected. I had no other mental recourse than to think that because I was Black and my car was a *Cop Magnet* that it was a tip-off to the officer that he had a good catch (someone who is likely to have an arrest warrant or the 3 No's – see Lesson 1, Instant Nolle p.2). I must say he was courteous, but very careless. I could only imagine what would have happened if I were not an officer myself.

That is why it is imperative that police officers have consideration for people and their families. I was glad that he did not put on his overhead emergency lights and hit the siren like police often do. That would have scared my kids and upset my wife. Moreover, it would have embarrassed me terribly.

Overall, the Lieutenant had his faults but he possessed an important asset to doing his job, consideration for the public.

Remember, in most cases, you will come out fine during almost any non-felony-related motor vehicle stop as long as you are courteous and polite. Don't try to be cute or a smart mouth, even if your parent or relative is a police officer, or your father is the chief of police, or you are the mayor's son.

The bottom line is during a motor vehicle investigation, the officer on scene will decide your fate based on his/her discretion and that will not be reviewed until a court date. By that time, you already will have been arrested, pepper sprayed or tazered. Some of you need to leave all of the homemade "street lawyer" debate for home or after the stop.

If talking is what you want to do, do it after the motor vehicle stop is over and you are well on your way. Call a friend and talk about it over the phone. However, if using a cell phone while driving is illegal in your state, then I suggest that you turn on your favorite song and relax.

So you are probably thinking that if a police officer pulls you over you have to just comply with whatever he says. Basically, yes! And know that police officers are not ruthless bandits searching for treasures like pirates. They are people working a job with a list of duties that are given to them. They have to show their superiors that they are working as well.

They just can't come to work and sit in the car all day wasting your tax dollars. In some departments, their budgets rely on motor vehicle stops that end with infraction tickets. In other departments, they won't turn down the prospect that motor vehicle infractions supplement their budget.

So when you get pulled over, it ain't personal. It's business!

This is what you should know regarding standard police conduct during motor vehicle stops.

TAKEN FROM STATE OF CONNECTICUT INFRACTION TICKET BOOK:

Because of reciprocity (whatever the status of your license and car registration is in any of the listed states, will be the same for all of the states listed), the same will stand for the following states as well:

- Alabama
- Alaska
- Arizona
- Arkansas
- California
- Colorado
- Connecticut
- Delaware
- District of Columbia
- Florida
- Georgia
- Hawaii
- Idaho
- Illinois
- Indiana
- Iowa
- Kansas
- Kentucky
- Louisiana
- Maine
- Maryland
- Massachusetts
- Minnesota
- Mississippi
- Missouri
- Montana
- Nebraska
- Nevada
- New Hampshire
- New Jersey
- New Mexico
- New York
- North Carolina
- North Dakota
- Ohio
- Oklahoma
- Oregon
- Pennsylvania
- Rhode Island
- South Carolina
- South Dakota
- Tennessee
- Texas
- Utah
- Vermont
- Virginia
- Washington
- West Virginia
- Wyoming

Links will lead to individual state pages.

INSTRUCTIONS TO OFFICERS

At all times be COURTEOUS, FAIR, and HONEST. Remember the public opinion of law enforcement is judged almost entirely by your (the officer's) conduct.

In issuing a complaint (ticket).

1. Introduce yourself to the accused by saying:
   "I am (give your rank, name and the enforcement agency you represent).

2. Ask for the driver's license and registration certificate or other identification.

3. Advise the accused of the offense committed.

4. Advise the accused that you are going to issue a complaint (ticket) for the offense(s).

5. Ask for any additional information necessary to fill out the complaint.

6. Fill out the complaint, have the accused sign the original and give the accused the proper copy along with an envelope. If the accused refuses to sign the original, print "REFUSED" on the signature line.

DO NOT- Lecture the accused.

DO NOT- Quiz the accused on knowledge of the law.

DO NOT- Indulge in personal remarks or altercations.

Schedule answer date for the second Friday after the date of the offense, even if such Friday is a holiday (may vary State to State).   --------------**End**-----------------

By you knowing what the officers guidelines are will not necessarily get you out of a traffic ticket, but it does serve as information that you can use as a guideline. Also, it gives you a better idea about the procedures of a motor vehicle stop. The bottom line is this, if you know that officers are given guidelines of behavior to follow during a stop, and then you should adopt the same type of philosophy or better.

The following suggested guidelines will significantly reduce you chances of getting a traffic ticket and will greatly reduce your risk of an arrest.

Recommended conduct for the Public during

Motor Vehicle Stops and encounters with police

<u>You should:</u>

- Be extra nice

- Be extra polite

- Be extra cooperative

- Be extra attentive

- Be honest (the police ain't stupid)

- Be extra respectful

- Don't fidget around or fumble about the car

- Roll down your window at least halfway

- Stay in your car unless ordered or asked to get out

- Have all of your paperwork in order

- Turn off your radio

- Turn off the car until the officer tells you to turn it on

- Don't get on the cell phone during the stop

- Don't try to intimidate the officer with whom you know

- Don't get mad when the officer gives you a ticket

- Don't talk back or try and get the last word in

- Use the same level of respect you would when talking with your grandparent

- Don't smoke a cigarette throughout the stop

Under the **circumstances of a non-felony motor vehicle stop**, if you follow those suggested guidelines you will significantly reduce you chances of getting a traffic ticket and will greatly reduce your risk of an arrest. Now let's be clear!

I'm not saying this is the secret to a "get out of jail free card."

If you have an outstanding arrest warrant, or if the motor vehicle stop was initiated under criminal circumstances, or if there are other issues involved in the stop beyond that of a motor vehicle stop, then you will probably be late for dinner. Nevertheless, you now have an idea of what you should be getting as far as quality assurance by the officer's service. Remember, police are public servants. But don't make the mistake and think they are like the waitress in a Denny's restaurant. Make that mistake and you won't make it twice.

Before you move onto the next lesson, I will give you an example of what you should say and do during a non-felony motor vehicle stop.

Example: When you see the police car turn on the emergency lights, you should begin to slow down. Sometimes there will be no lights. The officer may flick his headlights and give a burst on the air horn. That is the horn that sounds like the one on the fire truck. No matter what, slow down.

If the officer is pulling you over, from that point you will know. So start pulling over to the side of the road. Don't go nuts. Just pull the car over to the side of the road as soon as possible. The longer you drive, the more you increase the intensity of the motor vehicle stop.

Once the car comes to a stop, roll down your window, turn off the engine and leave the key in the ignition. Turn off the radio.

Don't move all around the car like you're cleaning up for a guest. Just keep your butt still and your hands in a location where they can easily be seen by the officer. Also, make eye contact with the officer. Don't look behind you to see where the officer is; believe me he's coming.

When the officer arrives at your car, he will most likely ask you right away "License and registration!"

You should reply, "Yes, officer! I would like to get it from my glove compartment." Or you may have it in a visor or in a compartment in the door. The bottom line is to say what you are about to do at all times, just like the game "Simon Says."

One Wrong Move

True Story: *One time I was stopped outside College Park in Georgia. At the time, I had my registration and insurance card in the trunk of the car inside of a duffle bag because I was unable to lock up my car. So when the officer came to the car he said, "I want you to give me your license and registration and insurance card!" He stood off from my window poised with his hand on his gun, ready to draw it on me. I was not stupid. I was definitely scared. During that time, its was 1989 "war on drugs." I was living in Georgia and was about 22 years old.*

So I stuttered and said to him "S----ir! M---y license is in my wallet that is in the gl---ove compartment." What he would say next was surely a "Pampers moment."

"Ok! I want you to reach into your glove compartment and get your wallet. And if you come out with anything other than that, you're gonna hear a loud pop! Ok!"

At that point I just wanted to confess, and the funny thing was, I had not done anything. But I was trying not to get shot!

You know what I'm saying? Nevertheless, I was not mad at the officer, probably because I was too doggone scared; anger was another emotion that I did not have room for anyway. Plus, at the end of the day, the officer had a job to do. However, he was an older guy, probably in his late 40s. And, as the stop progressed, he explained that my car fit the description of a car that had been involved in a triple homicide a few days ago. Ironically, when I had gone to the trunk to get my registration and stuff, the officer started back up again with that "pop talk" because he saw a camouflage duffle bag in the trunk. Well, I wasn't the guy so that was that. After he found out that I was a college student, he had normal conversation with me. I remember him having a sigh of relief as he told me how his heart had dropped when he saw the duffle bag in my car because the perpetrators had carried Mac-11 machine guns in a similar bag. "I was thanking God that there was nothing in your bag but tools and then I knew you were not their buddy!"

When you are initially stopped, you may have no room for a bunch of conversation. But by some chance if you can, you should get as much positive information in as possible. Such as "Officer, my name is Tyrone Little. I am a student at Tulane University and I was on my way to study at the library. I am sorry if I have caused you some inconvenience." By that time you should have gotten your license, registration and insurance cards together.

"Here, officer!" Make some eye contact and sit tight.

You may have a passenger(s) in the car and it is very important that you keep your passenger(s) under control. Why? A bad passenger can cost you a lot of money and points on your license. One reason is because when an officer stops you for a motor vehicle violation, he/she is really only concerned with what you did. But if you have a passenger who is getting smart and saying inappropriate things to the officer or is doing stupid stuff like interrupting the officer while he is talking, then your passenger will escalate what would have been a basic motor vehicle stop to an investigative detention in which you and your smarty pants passenger will both be on the verge of an arrest.

So what is the preferred behavior for a passenger? I suggest that all passengers follow the same procedures that I previously recommended for a driver. The exception being, the passenger does not have to volunteer information or identification unless he is asked. In the meantime he/she should remain calm and sit still. Sit still! Sit still! And keep his hands in an area in plain view of the officer. In addition, when the officer is talking to the driver, the passenger should be very attentive to what the officer is saying. And never turn around and look behind.

If you get a ticket

Now let's talk about what happens if you get a ticket, and most likely you will get one. In some cases, you may get a warning ticket or an inspection ticket, which will require you to go to the Department of Motor Vehicles within a 15-day period or so and prove that you have corrected the violation mentioned on the inspection ticket.

If you get either, I suggest that you do the following:

1. Rule number one, don't freak out!
2. Stay calm, cool and collected!
3. Don't argue with the officer or quiz him/her!
4. Don't show any attitude!
5. Remember that the officer is doing his or her job!
6. Don't say anything slick or sarcastic prior to pulling off!
7. Don't pull away fast causing your tires to screech!
8. Say "thank you" to the officer, and tell him that you are sorry that you caused him/her any inconvenience!

Make sure that you clearly understand what date deadlines you need to meet for the ticket and that you clearly understand the charges.

Don't debate the issue; "Officer, why did you charge me with *not stopping* at the stop sign? I stopped!"

This is definitely an example of what not to do. You will only prolong the stop and increase your chances to say or do something to get you locked up.

> **"Keep talking and you are likely to say something to get locked up!"**

About 99% of the time, that is what happens. Then you're in the back seat trying to tell the officer what his/her job description is. How you're a taxpayer and pay his salary. It just gets real ugly. So, don't get yourself in this position. Keep your big mouth closed. Also, don't ask the officer for his or her name and badge number. If the officer gives you a ticket it will be on the infraction. If you can't read it, call the police department and give them the case number, and they will be able to look up the information about the stop. All police departments have a database in which a record of every motor vehicle stop is recorded and stored. The record of the motor vehicle stop will show the officer's rank and name as well as the date and time of the stop.

In most states around the country, police cruisers have cameras. From the time the officer initiates the stop everything is being recorded. So again, pretend that your grandmother is following you. What would you do? How would you act? Seriously, think about it! Because should you decide to contest the ticket or take it to court, the prosecutor will be showing your silly butt *live and direct*. And for some reason you won't seem so cute looking at yourself 20 days later, early in the morning, when you're missing a day's pay from work and are about to pay a fine.

I have spent a lot of time on the issue of conduct during motor vehicle stops because the vast majority of you who encounter or meet police will meet them as a driver or passenger of a car. And if you know how to properly communicate with police officers during a motor vehicle stop, then you will have no problem communicating with them during most situations. Just remember most police use one basic philosophy.

> **"Treat me (the officer) with respect and I'll treat you with respect!"**

Lesson 4: Ma! You Ain't Helping!

When Family Comes on the Scene & Gets Locked Up Too

On countless occasions I have seen mothers, fathers, brothers, sisters, relatives, girlfriends, boyfriends, baby's momma, baby's daddy and guardians earn their way into a nice shining pair of handcuffs trying to so-called rescue some young Black or Hispanic/Latino male from being arrested. Understand this! If a police officer tells you that you're under arrest, then there is no negotiation.

In some cases, there might be room for debate, but you take a chance when you engage the officer as to "Why is my son in the car? Why is my son in handcuffs? Why is my son under arrest? He didn't do nothing!"

The reality is that protesting mothers, fathers, brothers, sisters, relatives, girlfriends, boyfriends, baby's momma, baby's daddy and guardians have come to the arrest scene two minutes or, in some cases, 15 minutes, after the police may have apprehended the young man (down the street) for crashing the stolen car. No! Mom does not see the stolen car or the injured person that her son hit with the car. Often this is because by the time the family arrives to verbally attempt to

70

free their relative; the car is one block away from the arrest scene. The injured victim has been transported to the hospital, and the other suspects involved have escaped on foot. Bottom line; your mom is too late!

But, with all of the yelling and cursing at the police, she is right on time for an arrest.

If you think it's a game, I know of a police officer whose mother was arrested by the very officers with whom he works with. She was arrested for engaging the police during the arrest of a family member and took a chance at cello police negotiation that is when you try to talk your way through what you know will ultimately be a situation that will cost you your life or freedom, but in your heart you hope that the officer shows his/her human side and looks beyond their own ego. The lieutenant in charge was brutal in his call to arrest the officer's mom, but it only proves the point that if an officer's mom can get arrested for challenging the police, you know your mom is going to jail. So next time, just tell your *peeps* to chill.

The Charges

In most states, it is considered *hindering* or *preventing* an officer from performing his/her duties as they pertain to his/her investigation at the time. Most often, it is a misdemeanor crime punishable by fine or very minimal incarceration. However, the effects can be long lasting in these incidents. Officers will use this as a proving point to the person that "you don't challenge us!"

Arrestees for these types of charges could find themselves with the highest allowable bond being set. They could also find their way to the bottom of the *processing order*, especially if they qualify for a PTA (Promise to Appear in court and no bail to be posted). They may sit in jail for five hours or more only to find out that they can leave with having to post a bail.

Case Report: Don't be the performing mother, father, brother, sister, relative, girl friend, boy friend, baby's momma, baby's daddy or guardian who tries to challenge the police to a *standoff breach*. I have witnessed thousands of incidents in which a young male committed a crime, often drug- or gun-related, that resulted in his arrest. He was in handcuffs and had been or was in the process of being searched for weapons or drugs. Normally the real guilty caught-red-handed types request that someone in the crowd call their mother.

It normally goes something like this:

"Yo, Laquisha, call my mother! Call my mother, yo! Tell her I ain't did nothing! Ah! Y'all (the police) get off of me! I ain't did nothing! D---mn! Yo! You hurtin' my arm!"

By this time, Laquisha is on the phone with the mother and mom is hearing all of the commotion in the background. Now keep in mind that today's generation of young males have fairly young mothers. They are often in their mid-thirties. That means it will not take mom long to show up to the scene, and she is coming with all of the street lawyer drama.

For some reason, when trying to communicate with the police, mothers of arrestees in particular think that they can use the same board-of-education-cuss-out techniques that they use with public school teachers. But understand one thing. Teachers have to stand there and listen to all of that nonsense. The police, however, have the option of discontinuing an unwanted conversation at any given time. Once they give the announcement, "Ma'am you need to step back onto the sidewalk! Or back up!" It is time to move out of the way and be quiet. You don't have to be completely silent. The key is to let the police know you are concerned about what happens to your relative and to do it in a way that does not antagonize the police. A loud mouth can incite a riot, and that can lead to an arrest, too.

And about those camcorders and camera phones – you need to understand one thing. Nothing, but nothing, will stop a police officer from arresting you. Once he/she has made up their mind, you are going to jail! Even if you took 30 minutes worth of arrest video and 30 pictures, your cousin, brother, father, etc. are going to jail! In addition, you may piss off the officers on scene and cause them to get more technical and add charges to the arrest that they may have normally left out.

For instance, say they were arresting your brother for a domestic violence dispute. His girlfriend said that he was arguing with her. So initially, the officers had determined that they were going to charge your brother with breach of peace. But then you break out the cameras and start with the *crazy talk*. Now the police re-examine the investigation and prompt the girlfriend about whether she felt threatened or if your brother said something threatening. Now the girlfriend, who just wanted to get rid of your brother, says that she was threatened and that he also grabbed her. "Did you feel pain?" the officer asks.

"Yes I did!" says the girlfriend.

Now the officers add threatening and assault charges to the breach of peace. All because you brought out the videos and cameras, along with the possibility that the event could be aired on the evening news and could set the stage for a possible lawsuit. So, the officer feels that he must now be extremely careful and exhaust all of his resources to make the arrest. Remember, an officer is not trained to lose.

Mom and Cops

True Story: *It was a rainy day. I was in a public park with another 16-year-old friend shooting at a squirrel in a tree with BB guns. Mine was a Daisy handgun, and his was a Daisy rifle. Needless to say, we were living in the inner city. In fact, I was less than a block from my house, and he was approximately two blocks from his house. Suddenly, a patrol officer casually pulled up in his cruiser. My friend took off running, but I stayed and explained to the officer what we were doing. He took my BB gun and told me to stay there until he got back. He then took off after my friend, who was running and jumping the fence in the park, carrying the gun the whole way.*

Well, I was not going to hang around to get in trouble. I casually left, walking en route to my house. I took the long way walking. On the way, I took off my jacket and hat and tucked them under my arm in case the police could not catch my friend, and they came looking for me. After about 15 minutes, I arrived home. I was soaking and wet, because I had been out in the rain most of the day playing with the BB gun in the woods. I liked to go

outside on rainy days. However, to my dismay, I arrived home to find my father had been drinking, and my mother was home. I knew that the police were going to find my house, so I immediately changed out of my wet clothes. There was a knock at the door as I began to explain to my un-sober father what had happened. It was the police. Actually, it was about four officers, and they had sent officers to the back of my door, as I could see them from my bedroom sliding glass door. I came out of my room. They were already in the house. I was under arrest, and now *Official Public Enemy #1*, some proud officer's collar of the day (accredited arrest that enhanced an officer's chances of promotion).

Well, my mother also arrived as they were taking me out. She flipped. She was mad, and I was more worried about her going to jail than I was about going myself. She cussed, fussed and yelled the entire time. Then she followed us in the "paddy wagon" (prisoner conveyance van) all the way to the station. All for a BB gun; my friend who ran got beat up once he was caught. He had made the police run and was 16 years old.

He broke the Golden Rule – never make the Police run!

When I arrived at the police station, I was placed in a holding area. The room was cinder blockabout the size of a typical bathroom in a house. It had a very high ceiling. All of the walls were painted a dingy yellow. The door was solid steel with a small wire mesh glass window, which had smudges of bloodstains and dried spit. There was profanity written on most of the walls. Someone had even written a phrase in blood. The room itself had the foul stench of urine. There were dried puddles of urine in the back of the room as well. It was so filthy that I did not touch anything. The room was cold, and I could not hear anything on the other side of the door. I felt helpless and hopeless. I kept thinking that I would never be able to escape this new environment, and I worried about how I would survive. After I was processed, I was put in a cell with my friend. He was doing push-ups because he said that he needed to prepare himself for jail. I stood up the entire time, because I did not even want to get used to being there. Plus, I knew my mother was at the station, and she was definitely going to get me out. The guard came by and offered us milk because we had just missed dinner. I refused to eat or drink anything. I felt that by doing so, I would have accepted being there, like the foot in the *door technique in psychology. I knew that if they had kept me, I would have starved to death. After about an hour, I was released on a PTA (promise to appear in court). My mother was not mad at me about the incident, but she was furious as hell towards the police - all police.*

I was not as mad about the incident as I was disappointed in the manner in which my parents, my friend, and I were treated. It showed me that, there was basically no respect for Black people when it came to the law. We were not "complete citizens," but my parents were property owners and hired our family lawyer. When I went to court, the charges were dropped. The next time I would see the inside of the prisoner holding area would be 14 years later when I was in the police academy touring the facility as part of my training. Ironically, our tour was shortened because someone had hung himself inside one of the cells. He was discovered by some of my fellow academy officers when we entered the cell hallway.

The lesson from this story is that, looking back over 25 years ago, my mother was very good in the way she conducted herself. Throughout the incident, she let the officers know that all she was concerned about was my safety. She did not focus on the reason for my arrest. I could remember her yelling. "He's a good kid! He's a Notre Dame student!" Comments like that are helpful in reminding officers with whom they are dealing. Understand that often police can develop *cultural tunnel vision* in which they are blinded by the content of their job. They will make comments like, "Why bother? Helping these people is like going to Hell in a hand basket." So, when you make comments that qualify or defend the arrestee's character, it often helps officers to re-focus and break out of their own zone.

Do not make the fatal mistake of trying to personalize the issue by asking the officer about their personal life.

"Officer, do you have kids?"

"Officer, do you have a wife/husband?"

"Officer, would you treat your mother like that?"

Trust me! Leave that stuff out. What will most likely happen is that you will draw the officer into a one-on-one argument that will result in you going to jail and the officer upping the charges on your relative. In addition, you may wind up saying something really stupid that will follow you back and forth to court. By asking questions like this, or making comments/statements like this, you make it personal. At least that is the way the officer will most likely take it.

If you plan to follow the paddy wagon or prisoner transport van down to the station, it is best not to make a big public announcement. Just ask the most calm-looking officer which precinct or station they are going to and how long they think it will be before your relative is processed and issued a bond. Also, ask for the telephone number to the booking desk officer or detention officer. Before you go, call your lawyer or bondsman, give them the scenario, and ask them what should you do next.

One of the other major mistakes you can make as a relative is to follow the police car if the officer is transporting the prisoner in the police cruiser. That is a very good way to get yourself arrested or possibly hurt. Remember, there are very few incidents in which arrestees have been injured or assaulted by police during transport to detention or the jailhouse. When you follow them, you create a risk to the public. You escalate the level of threat to the officers involved in transporting the person. And the bottom line, you ain't helpin'! So don't do it.

> **If the ultimate goal is to help your "peeps" get out of jail faster, you will have a hard time doing it if you're in jail with them!**

Conclusion

Hold Your Fire – Instant Justice

There is no doubt in my mind that the advice that I have provided to you in this book will prevent many unwanted and unnecessary incidents between American law enforcement and various cultural groups within the urban sector. And if, you were able to benefit from one word that was offered, then it was worth the effort for me to compile the information. While writing this book, many of my colleagues and friends questioned rather or not this topic would be a good idea (safe topic) for me to write about. Others question if this subject would jeopardize my safety and career opportunities in the field of law enforcement.

As a police officer who has worked in the urban sector for over 13 years, I believe that many of the situations that young Black, Hispanic and Latino males find themselves in are created or guided by many of their own mishaps. It may be intentional: "I'm gonna let them (the police) know what's up." Or it may be unintentional: "Why am I being held at gunpoint for a broken tail light?" As an officer who watches this drama unfold on a daily basis, I felt compelled to offer some insight as to what we as citizens and law enforcement officers can do to prevent and diffuse these contentious incidents, which often result in the officer using some level of force. In some cases, extreme deadly force is used, like the Sean Bell shooting in

Queens, New York, in which officers fired a total of 50 bullets to stop an unarmed Black male driver. One of the officers alone fired over 31 bullets. Understand incidents like this do not occur because of a misunderstanding or a mistaken identity. Incidents like this, as well as the ones sited earlier in Lesson 2 (page 28), happen because of an officer's inability to identify, understand, and effectively communicate with a specific population (commonly Black) within the urban sectors of the United States.

Let's face it. Rodney King (Los Angeles, California), Malik Jones (New Haven, Connecticut), Abner Louima (Fatbush, New York), Franklyn Reid (New Milford, Connecticut), Aqhmed Amadu Diallo (New York), Aquan Salmon (Hartford, Connecticut), Patrick Dorismond (Manhattan, New York), Sean Bell (Queens, New York)… and the list goes on and will go on – all of these incidents occurred within the geographical limits of the urban sector. You call it the inner city. The reality is that these incidents almost never take place in the rural areas or the suburbs. Why? I'll tell you why. It is because of the perception of law enforcement. That same perception is often left to the assumptions of the officer who will use it as a major tool in "Officer Discretional Powers." The problem is that discretion is like a sword in an officer's hand. If the officer is weak, he will wield a weak sword and if the officer is strong, he will wield a strong sword. The only way these two officers will be able to wield their swords any differently is if they are trained to do so by someone who is an expert on the subject and can teach them. This is not rocket science, but it is not "because the police has a badge, they know it all." No, we don't know it all. In fact, we rely on you and the rest of society to help us come to a conclusion on 50% of the incidents that we encounter. The public knowing how to properly communicate with officers will serve as a major tool when you are dealing with law enforcement.

One of my favorite authors, Franz Fannon, does an excellent job and describing the mindset of police during this *era of urban police violence.* In his book, Master Slave Paradigm he wrote:

"Those who monopolize and benefit from violence as a necessary, justified and for the good of all. The opportunities are permitted no right of self-defense, no due process of law. But the policemen who, unprovoked/shoots one of the oppressed or breaks heads with batons is likely to be hailed as the protector of justice, the defender of law and order."

I am all but truly disgusted with the recent police shooting in Queens, New York. Again, we are trying to figure out how another unarmed young male, who coincidently has dark-colored skin, is the victim of excessive talk and long, drawn-out meetings. In my opinion, that is what played the key role in the estimated 50 bullets that officers fired in fear of their lives. Sean Bell was not shot because he was "driving while Black." He was not shot because he was on *"America's Most Wanted."*

He was shot because many of us in the urban sector spend too much time talking about what needs to be done instead of doing it. We worry about what the church is not doing. We worry about what the community leaders are not doing. We worry about what the educators are not doing. All this time is wasted trying to assess blame. And now, our blame has turned to shame.

The disturbing issue in this incident is that no one seems to know why this shooting occurred. Sure, it is evident that there was some type of investigation going on. Was it an undercover operation gone bad? It would not have been the first one in New York City and, from my research, it most likely will not be the last.

Historically, America's mistreatment of minorities by the police in the urban sector existed long before 1950 and 1960.

The epitome of America's mistreatment of minorities in the urban sectors of America by law enforcement took place on East Street in Harlem, New York, in July 1917[2]. That riot would leave over 200 Black people dead and over 6,000 homeless. The world renowned Black female performing artist Josephine Baker responded to the incident with these harsh words: "The very idea of America makes me shake and tremble and gives me nightmares." She went on to live most of the rest of her life exiled in France. No longer could Blacks continue with the myth that only cops in the South hated Black people.

In addition to the civil rights issues and protests, America was faced with the failures from the "War on Poverty." Frustrated Blacks and oppressed residents of ghettos had resorted to violence and insisted that it was the constant police brutality that had contributed to the countless number of riots. White candidates running for governmental offices used "law and order" and better armed control of the ghetto as an election ploy. Police departments ordered new and more powerful weapons to meet ghetto "trouble." In 1968, Mayor Richard Daley of Chicago and Gomuo Spiro Agnew of Maryland issued "shoot to kill" orders to law enforcement officers. History now repeating itself as many urban departments are re-arming their departments.

---

[2] Kats, William Loren. *Eyewitness: The Negro in American History A Living Documentary Of The Afro-American,* New York, Toronto, London: Pitman Publishing Corporation 1967, 1971.

This new direction in American law enforcement hinders our social structure in the urban sector from reaching its cultural potential. *Deadly Force* has been this newer tool added to the officer's disposal and it's a tool without clear instructions. "When do I shoot?" "When is too many shots too many?" As an officer who has been involved in police-related shootings involving Black and Hispanic males, I can say when you only have two seconds to decide, it's tough. And you are often left to "what you know in your heart." And it's that "right thing" is based on your interpretation of the people with whom you are engaging or dealing. The problem occurs when it does not add up and steps are not taken to fix the problem. Being shot to death for being in and leaving a strip club? Since when did having a bachelor party become a felony? The shooting of Sean Bell is a problem, and a big one at that. When we look at past incidents involving the treatment of urban males in New York, instead of carrying out the hundreds of resolutions that piled up, we continued to meet. Meeting is safe. Yet safe for who?

Let's not forget while we were meeting in August 9, 1997, in Flatbush, New York City a group of officers sexually assaulted a Haitian male (again, a young Black male) who had been arrested at a night club for charges that could have been addressed by using a misdemeanor summons ticket and by giving him a Promise to Appear in court. Evidence later presented showed that the officers inserted a 14-inch broken stick/plunger into the anus of the subject and then removed the stick and shoved it into the subject's mouth.

Then again, on February 4, 1999, America would see unchanged law enforcement and racial profiling at its finest. A group of white cops (who were undercover and dressed in plain clothes) shot an unarmed Muslim male from Guinea, while he stood in the foyer of his apartment building getting his keys or wallet from his pocket. The four cops shot at him a horrific 41 times and the African-born Muslim male was struck by gunfire 19 times. What started out with a subject fitting the description ended in a positive identification of the state of America's outlook on urban men.

And while we were meeting and planning how to prevent these now three major tragedies from recurring, on March 16, 2000, in midtown Manhattan, New York, another undercover op gone bad would result in the fatal shooting of another Black male who was suspected of possibly having or wanting a small amount of drugs. In this incident, the twist was that the cop was Hispanic and the shooting happened in an upscale area rather than the inner city. Once again, the suspect was unarmed. Moreover, like the previously mentioned NYPD shooting, the suspect was mistaken for someone else and was innocent. Sounds like a war? And this is only a snapshot look at some of the actions and results of actions that have involved police and the public since 1996 in the tri-state area. The irony is that in all of the incidents that I have highlighted, all of the subjects killed or severely assaulted were unarmed and no weapons were recovered at the scene. In addition, they were all Black males or urban males.

The bottom line is that there is no time to meet. As my dear friend and New Haven Community Activist Doug Bethea says, "we are going to die in meetings!" Except in these cases, other people died while we were in meetings accomplishing nothing. The main ingredient to improving the relationship between law enforcement and the members of the urban community is education, knowledge, and decisive and swift action. An officer's knowledge of the *ethnic colloquialism-* lifestyles, and body language of Black and Hispanic people who live in the inner city, can and will make a difference in the officer's success when working in that urban environment and can also play a major role in effectuating this positive change in police-community relations.

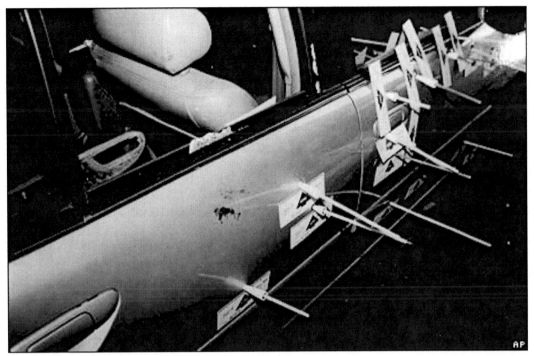

Shown above is a photo of the car Sean Bell was driving when police officers fired a total of 50 shots at the car - 31 by just one officer. This photo shows where the bullets entered the vehicle.

Many law enforcement officers feel that it's the knowledge of the streets that gives an officer that "special edge." This knowledge is gained through an officer's training and experience from working in the field. In most cases, the "field" is the job environment where the suspects live and dwell. However, street knowledge is not just developed through working by patrolling the streets in a given neighborhood or community. Officers must set out to earn the trust and confidence of the people they serve in that area. "Actions are judged by intentions." I intend to help the people who live in these inner city neighborhoods. It is not just because of the money the officer earns, but because he has a sincere desire to help others. With this as the premise prior to the start of each work day, night, or even at the beginning of a career, it will lead to a role of establishing a productive relationship with the people and that community. I use the word "productive" relationship and not the overused and un-represented term, "positive." It seems as though the word "positive" has been overused, especially when it is used in conjunction with causes for Blacks and Hispanic/Latinos.

Police and other law enforcement officers are held to a high standard. But, what we must never forget is that these officers are the same individuals who come from our imperfect society. That's right, many people expect the police to be perfect, but we hope that they are really imperfect, especially when it could result in one of our relatives or friends beating a court case or wining a million dollar brutality suit.

We want to hold them accountable and blame them for all of our problems as well as the problems of other people. If I have no hot water because my landlord refused to fix the pipes, once the police arrive I expect that this problem will be solved. If my baby's daddy won't pay child support, once the police come I expect that the problem will be fixed, for next month too. And once the officer has explained to them (as I have done many times) that these are civil law matters (like on Judge Judy or Judge Joe Brown or Judge Mathis), they become even angrier with the officer because they feel that their tax dollars pay police officers to serve all of their needs. Often, I have to explain to people that an officer's ability is limited and that some policies can only be changed through the Mayor at City Hall or the Governor or other elected officials. Often, they become very frustrated and vent. Unfortunately, the officer is the one who becomes the outlet.

Moreover, this is one of the big problems with community-based policing: The people/citizens/residents become grossly dependent upon law enforcement to manage their daily affairs. They expect that the police will offer a solution to their very complex social needs.

The reality is that the police are better equipped to fulfill that duty than one of the state or city agencies assigned to address the problem. Under this new policing concept of "getting police closer to the people they serve," store owners get greedy and want the police to themselves. They want the homeless people to be removed from in front of their store, and they don't care if they get arrested or go to 24-hour drug rehabilitation center. Just so long as they are removed from infront of their place of business.

When the City seeks to get big corporations to relocate to regentrified parts of the city, once known as the blighted housing areas, the city officials give a "green light to lock *them* up, if they are hanging out." An officer can report for duty, be given instructions to "crack down on the corners," conduct numerous field interviews, take names, give out loitering tickets, and make arrests. This is often known as "kicking a...es and taking names." This translates into a 16-hour police state. Then, after 2000 or so arrests and one year later, the buildings come down. The streets are dug up and paved, and the street's direction of travel even changed. The sidewalks and curbs are replaced. The city's building inspection department steps in and closes the corner stores that have harbored drug operations, drug paraphernalia, and drug dealers for years. In fact, there is nothing familiar to the area anymore except the presence of the police, whose duty it is to now protect the investment property from damage, vandalism, and burglary.

So, what will be the criterion for the next generation of officers if the majority of citizens they serve will be affiliates of big corporations and private industry? Will training on race relations become extinct and sensitivity training obsolete? Will vital walking beat be replaced by mobile beats that will deter officers from establishing personal relationships with youth and other community members? And will this change in training allow officers who have their own agenda as a cop to become the majority among the ones in whom the public entrust their safety? I hope not!

There is a real problem going on in the *world of policing*, and we as an American society need to fix it right a way. We have an enormous task already trying to solve gun violence and other violent crimes among our teenage youth and young adults nationwide. How can we expect to guide them in issues of interpersonal conflict, when we have not resolved our misconceptions and misperceptions about other cultures? We are of many different cultures, but we all are of but one race, the human race, and that is the culture of harmony.

In 2009, we have a failing economy. President Barack Hussein Obama said in his first presidential address on February 9, 2009, that our economy is the worst it has ever been since the Great Depression. And history has shown that a failing economy go hand and hand with an increase in criminal activity. The gun violence epidemic in America is out of control, gangs on the rise, war on drugs a failed fairy tale in the poppy fields of Afghanistan, and police contacts with the public will become more confrontational. As a result, police shootings will increase likely increase. Based on the previous pattern of police related shootings, incidents will most likely occur in the urban sector among young Black and Hispanic/Latin males.

"The Beginning of the Truth and the End to Lies."

Tell me what topics and concerns you would like me to write about the next book.

Log on to **WWW.AblackMansGuideToLawEnforcementInAmerica.com**

Bonus Resource Material

The following information was produced by the American Civil Liberties Union. It can also be found on the ACLU website aclu.org/profiling www.aclu.org.

Everyone, including minors, has the right to courteous and respectful police treatment. If your rights are violated, don't try to deal with the situation at the scene. You can talk to a lawyer afterwards, or file a complaint with the Internal Affairs or Civilian Complaint Board.

What to Do if You're Stopped by the Police

- Think carefully about your words, movement, body language, and emotions.
- Don't get into an argument with the police.
- Remember, anything you say or do can be used against you.
- Keep your hands where the police can see them.
- Don't run. Don't touch any police officer.
- Don't resist even if you believe you are innocent.
- Don't complain on the scene or tell the police they're wrong or that you're going to file a complaint.
- Do not make any statements regarding the incident.
- Ask for a lawyer immediately upon your arrest.

■ Remember officers' badge and patrol car numbers.

■ Write down everything you remember ASAP.

■ Try to find witnesses and obtain their names and phone numbers.

■ If you are injured, take photographs of the injuries as soon as possible, but make sure you seek medical attention first.

■ If you feel your rights have been violated, file a written complaint with police department's internal affairs division or civilian complaint board, or call the ACLU hotline, 1-877-6-PROFILE.

If You're Stopped in Your Car

1. Upon request, show the officer your driver's license, registration, and proof of insurance. In certain cases, your car can be searched without a warrant as long as the police have probable cause. To protect yourself later, you should make it clear that you do not consent to a search. It is not lawful for police to arrest you simply for refusing to consent to a search.

2. If you're given a ticket, you should sign it; otherwise you can be arrested. You can always fight the case in court later.

3. If you're suspected of drunk driving (DWI) and refuse to take a blood, urine or breath test, your driver's license may be suspended.

If You're Arrested or Taken to a Police Station

1. You have the right to remain silent and to talk to a lawyer before you talk to the police. Tell the police nothing except your name and address. Don't give any explanations, excuses or stories. You can make your defense later, in court, based on what you and your lawyer decides is best.

2. Ask to see a lawyer immediately. If you can't pay for a lawyer, you have a right to a free one, and should ask the police how the lawyer can be contacted. Don't say anything without a lawyer.

3. Within a reasonable time after your arrest or booking, you have the right to make a local phone call: to a lawyer, bail bondsman, a relative or any other person. The police may not listen to the call to the lawyer.

4. Sometimes you can be released without bail, or have bail lowered. Have your lawyer ask the judge about this possibility. You must be taken before the judge on the next court day after arrest.

5. Do not make any decisions in your case until you have talked with a lawyer.

In Your Home

1. If the police knock and ask to enter your home, you don't have to admit them unless they have a warrant signed by a judge.

2. However, in some emergency situations (like when a person is screaming for help inside, or when the police are chasing someone) officers are allowed to enter and search your home without a warrant.

3. If you are arrested, the police can search you and the area close by. If you are in a building, "close by" usually means just the room you are in. We all recognize the need for effective law enforcement, but we should also understand our own rights and responsibilities – especially in our relationships with the police.

Arrest the Racism

Tell us about your race- or ethnic-based traffic or pedestrian stop. Call 1-877-6-PROFILE or go to aclu.org/profiling www.aclu.org

1. What you say to the police is always important. What you say can be used against you, and it can give the police an excuse to arrest you, especially if you bad-mouth a police officer.

2. You must show your driver's license and registration when you are stopped in a car. Otherwise, you don't

have to answer any questions if you are detained or arrested, with one important exception. The police may ask for your name if you have been properly detained, and you can be arrested in some states for refusing to give it. If you reasonably fear that your name is incriminating, you can claim the right to remain silent, which may be a defense in case you are arrested anyway.

3. You don't have to consent to any search of yourself, your car or your house. If you do consent to a search, it can affect your rights later in court. If the police say they have a search warrant, ask to see it.

4. Do not interfere with, or obstruct the police – you can be arrested for it.

If You are Stopped for Questioning

1. It's not a crime to refuse to answer questions, but refusing to answer might make the police suspicious about you. If you are asked to identify yourself, see paragraph 2 above.

2. Police may "pat-down" your clothing if they suspect a concealed weapon. Don't physically resist, but make it clear that you don't consent to any further search.

3. Ask if you are under arrest. If you are, you have a right to know why.

4. Don't bad-mouth the police officer or run away, even if you believe what is happening is unreasonable. That could lead to your arrest.

The following information was produced by the Virginia Beach Police Department. It can also be found on the Virginia Beach website at:

http://www.vbgov.com/dept/police/

Virginia Beach Police Department Headquarters

Municipal Center – Building 11

2509 Princess Anne Road

Virginia Beach, Virginia 23456

Virginia Beach Police Mission Statement

The Virginia Beach Police Department is committed to providing a safe community and improving the quality of life for all people. We accomplish this by delivering quality police services and enforcing laws with equity and impartiality. In partnership with the community, we reduce crime through public education, prevention, and awareness. In meeting this objective, we demand of ourselves the highest professional standards and dedication to our core values.

Why You Could be Stopped by the Police:

There are many different reasons why the police can legally stop you:

- You may have committed a traffic violation.

- You, your passenger, or the vehicle you are driving may fit the description of an individual and/or vehicle wanted for a crime.

- The officer might think you need help. If you are stopped by the police while driving, you may feel confused, anxious, or even angry. These are natural feelings, but remember, traffic stops are stressful and dangerous for the officer. Each year a number of police officers are killed or seriously injured while making a "routine" traffic stop. Police officers are especially vulnerable during hours of darkness. With this in mind, there are things that you, as a law-abiding citizen, can do to help lessen the potential for unpleasantness during the stop.

Remember!

In all cases, citizens are asked to cooperate with police officers.

When Stopped by the Police

- A police officer may pull you over at any time for a traffic offense or criminal police investigation.

- When you observe an officer behind you with emergency lights and/or siren activated, remain calm and safely pull over to the right side of the road.

- Remain in your vehicle unless the officer advises you otherwise.

- Keep your hands in plain sight so the officer can see them.

- Avoid any sudden movements, especially toward the floorboard, rear seat, or passenger side of the vehicle.

- If the stop occurs at night, the officer will most likely illuminate the inside of your vehicle with spotlights. This is for the officer's safety as well as your own. Activating the interior or dome light of your vehicle will assist the officer in this regard.

- If there are passengers in your vehicle, encourage them to remain quiet and cooperate with the officer's instructions. The officer has a legal right to detain both the driver and occupants of a stopped vehicle.

- Wait until the officer asks for your driver's license, vehicle registration, or other documents before reaching for them. If the documents are out of reach, inform the officer where they are located before reaching for them.

- It is not unusual to see two or more police cars at the scene of a traffic stop.
- Do not touch or run from a police officer.
- Don't resist an arrest, even if you believe that you are innocent.
- The officer may issue you a ticket. If you feel the reason is vague or unclear, ask the officer for clarification.
- If you receive a ticket, signing it only means you promise to appear in court. Signing the ticket is not an admission of guilt.
- Avoid becoming argumentative. If you desire to contest the ticket, you will have an opportunity to address the matter in court.

Each stop made by a police officer is different, and the officer will adjust his or her response to fit the circumstances.

Police Officers:

- Will present proper identification if he or she is not in uniform. You may request to examine the identification so that you are satisfied that they are a police officer.
- Will inform you of the reason for the stop.
- Will not search the body of the opposite sex except to prevent injury to the officer or another person or to prevent the disposal or destruction of evidence.
- Will provide his or her name upon request.

Questions/Compliments/Complaints

If you have a question about the procedures or a complaint about the way you were treated, contact the Professional Standards Office or the officer's precinct and ask to speak with a supervisor. You may send a letter of appreciation if you feel the officer was particularly helpful or treated you fairly during your encounter. This information brochure has been published in hopes of providing answers to common questions about traffic stop procedures. With this information, it is hoped that the anxiety and stress you may feel, if stopped by the police, can be reduced.

A. M. Jacocks, Jr. - Chief of Police

Virginia State Code S 46.2-829

Requires that upon the approach of an emergency vehicle, drivers of other vehicles shall, as quickly as traffic and other highway conditions permit, drive to the nearest edge of the roadway, clear of any intersection, and stop and remain stopped, unless otherwise directed by a law enforcement officer, until the emergency vehicle has passed.

For further information you may contact the precinct in which you were stopped and ask to speak with a supervisor.

First Precinct & Special Operations
Municipal Center Building 11
2509 Princess Anne Road
Virginia Beach, VA 23456
(757) 427-4377 (1st), (757) 427-4606 (SO)

Second Precinct (Oceanfront area)
820 Virginia Beach Boulevard
Virginia Beach, VA 23451
(757) 437-7660

Third Precinct (Bayside area)
926 Independence Boulevard
Virginia Beach, VA 23455
(757) 219-2703

Fourth Precinct (Kempsville area)
840 Kempsville Road
Virginia Beach, VA 23464
(757) 474-8500

Professional Standards Office
Municipal Center, Building 11
2509 Princess Anne Road
Virginia Beach, VA 23456
(757) 427-4145

For more information, please visit the Virginia

Beach Police Department's web site at

http://www.vbgov.com/dept/police

Additional Resources

National Black Police Association

3251 Mt. Pleasant Street, N.W. Second Floor

Washington, DC 20010-2103

(202) 986-2070   (202) 986-0410 FAX

Virginia Beach Police Department Headquarters

A. M. Jacocks, Jr. - Chief of Police

Municipal Center – Building 11

2509 Princess Anne Road, Virginia Beach, Virginia 23456

http://www.vbgov.com/dept/police/

First Precinct & Special Operations

Municipal Center Building 11

2509 Princess Anne Road

Virginia Beach, VA 23456

(757) 427-4377 (1st)

(757) 427-4606 (SO)

Second Precinct (Oceanfront area)

820 Virginia Beach Boulevard

Virginia Beach, VA 23451

(757) 437-7660

Third Precinct (Bayside area)

926 Independence Boulevard

Virginia Beach, VA 23455

(757) 219-2703

Fourth Precinct (Kempsville area)

840 Kempsville Road

Virginia Beach, VA 23464

(757) 474-8500

Professional Standards Office
Municipal Center, Building 11

2509 Princess Anne Road

Virginia Beach, VA 23456

(757) 427-4145

U.S. Department of Justice Office of
Community Oriented Policing Services

The following has been taken from the US Department of Justice Office of Community Oriented Policing Services Website at www.ojp.usdoj.gov/

Who We Are: The COPS Office was created as a result of the Violent Crime Control and Law Enforcement Act of 1994.

As a component of the Justice Department, the mission of the COPS Office is to advance community policing in jurisdictions of all sizes across the country. Community policing represents a shift from more traditional law enforcement in that it focuses on prevention of crime and the fear of crime on a very local basis. Community policing puts law enforcement professionals on the streets and assigns them a beat, so they can build mutually beneficial relationships with the people they serve. By earning the trust of the members of their communities and making those individuals stakeholders in their own safety, community policing makes law enforcement safer and more efficient, and makes America safer.

What We Do: COPS provides grants to tribal, state, and local law enforcement agencies to hire and train community policing professionals, acquire and deploy cutting-edge crime-fighting technologies, and develop and test innovative policing strategies. COPS-funded training helps advance community policing at all levels of law enforcement - from line officers to law enforcement executives - as well as others in the criminal justice field. Because community policing is by definition inclusive, COPS training also reaches state and local government leaders and the citizens they serve. This broad range of programs helps COPS offer agencies support in virtually every aspect of law enforcement, and it's making America safer, one neighborhood at a time.

COPS has invested $11.3 billion to add community policing officers to the nation's streets and schools, enhance crime-fighting technology, support crime prevention initiatives, and provide training and technical assistance to advance community policing.

At of the end of fiscal year 2004, COPS funded more than 118,768 community policing officers and deputies.

U.S. Department of Justice
Office of Community Oriented Policing Services
1100 Vermont Avenue, NW

Washington, DC 20530

Response Center: 800.421.6770 or 202.307.1480

askCopsRC@usdoj.gov

The American Civil Liberties Union

The following has been taken from the ACLU website at http://www.aclu.org.

The American system of government is founded on two counterbalancing principles: that the majority of the people governs, through democratically elected representatives; and that the power even of a democratic majority must be limited, to ensure individual rights.

Majority power is limited by the Constitution's Bill of Rights, which consists of the original ten amendments ratified in 1791, plus the three post-Civil War amendments (the 13th, 14th and 15th) and the 19th Amendment (women's suffrage), adopted in 1920.

The mission of the ACLU is to preserve all of these protections and guarantees:

- Your First Amendment rights-freedom of speech, association and assembly. Freedom of the press, and freedom of religion supported by the strict separation of church and state.
- Your right to equal protection under the law - equal treatment regardless of race, sex, religion or national origin.
- Your right to due process - fair treatment by the government whenever the loss of your liberty or property is at stake.

- Your right to privacy - freedom from unwarranted government intrusion into your personal and private affairs.

We work also to extend rights to segments of our population that have traditionally been denied their rights, including Native Americans and other people of color; lesbians, gay men, bisexuals and transgender people; women; mental-health patients; prisoners; people with disabilities; and the poor. If the rights of society's most vulnerable members are denied, everybody's rights are imperiled.

The ACLU was founded by Roger Baldwin, Crystal Eastman, Albert DeSilver and others in 1920. We are nonprofit and nonpartisan and have grown from a roomful of civil liberties activists to an organization of more than 500,000 members and supporters. We handle nearly 6,000 court cases annually from our offices in almost every state.

The ACLU has maintained the position that civil liberties must be respected, even in times of national emergency. The ACLU is supported by annual dues and contributions from its members, plus grants from private foundations and individuals. We do not receive any government funding.

The National Lawyers Guild

The following is taken from the National Lawyers Guild website at http://www.nlg.org/

The **National Lawyers Guild** is dedicated to the need for basic and progressive change in the structure of our political and economic system. Through its members--lawyers, law students, jailhouse lawyers and legal workers united in chapters and committees—the Guild works locally, nationally and internationally as an effective political and social force in the service of the people.

Our aims:

- to eliminate racism;
- to safeguard and strengthen the rights of workers, women, farmers and minority groups, upon whom the welfare of the entire nation depends;
- to maintain and protect our civil rights and liberties in the face of persistent attacks upon them;
- to use the law as an instrument for the protection of the people, rather than for their repression.

"...to the end that human rights shall be regarded as more sacred than property interests."

The Institute for Justice: http://www.ij.org/

Institute Profile: Who We Are: Founded in 1991, the Institute for Justice is what a civil liberties law firm should be. As our nation's only libertarian public interest law firm, we pursue cutting-edge litigation in the courts of law and in the court of public opinion on behalf of individuals whose most basic rights are denied by the government—like the right to earn an honest living, private property rights, and the right to free speech, especially in the areas of commercial and Internet speech. As *Wired* magazine said, the Institute for Justice "helps individuals subject to wacky government regulations."

Simply put, we sue the government when it stands in the way of people trying to earn an honest living, when it unconstitutionally takes away individuals' property, when bureaucrats instead of parents dictate the education of children, and when government stifles speech. We seek a rule of law under which individuals can control their destinies as free and responsible members of society.

We have accomplished a great deal since our founding in 1991. You may have seen our clients, cases and attorneys featured frequently in the national media, such as ABC News *20/20* or the CBS News program *60 Minutes.* As *Investor's Business Daily* observed, "The Institute for Justice's influence is being felt across the nation."

The Institute for Justice is a 501(c)(3) organization; **contributions** are tax-deductible.

National Lawyers Guild Institute Mission:

Through strategic litigation, training, communication and outreach, the Institute for Justice advances a rule of law under which individuals can control their destinies as free and responsible members of society. IJ litigates to secure economic liberty, school choice, private property rights, freedom of speech and other vital individual liberties and to restore constitutional limits on the power of government. In addition, IJ trains law students, lawyers and policy activists in the tactics of public interest litigation. Through these activities, IJ challenges the ideology of the welfare state and illustrates and extends the benefits of freedom to those whose full enjoyment of liberty is denied by government.

About the Book

As a police officer who is currently employed in the New England area of the United States, I intend to provide a reliable publication that can be used as a learning tool to educate the general public about police and to educate police and other law enforcement officers (present and future) about the historical and social disposition of the people they are sworn to *protect and serve.*

This book is by no means pro-cop or anti-police and should not to be used as a literary pawn in cultural warfare (data for the self proclaimed leaders who seek to elevate their status in our society by disguising truth with rhetoric and conjecture). However, it is intended to provoke deep personal reflection and a critical analysis on the outlook of policing in America and its past, present and future impact on the day-to-day lives of those who live in America. This refers to all American citizens, both native and naturalized. It also refers to people who temporarily reside in the U.S., such as people awaiting green cards and illegal immigrants, not diplomats.

If you find this book enjoyable and informative after completely reading it, don't worry. There'll be another. However, if after completely reading it you got mad as hell, get ready, because it's only the beginning!

May God, the Creator of the Heavens and the Earth and all of Man, Jins, and Angels, bless the souls of all those who have died in the cause of making this United States of America a better place to live for every man, woman, and child. And may He also watch over the families of all those Law Enforcement Officers who lost their lives in the line of duty.

Amen

Shafiq R. F. Abdussabur

About the Author

Shafiq R.F. Abdussabur is an active law enforcement officer in the State of Connecticut with over 14 years of Community Base Police training and experience. He has been working with Inner City Youth since 1985. He is native of New Haven, Connecticut having grown up in various sections of the urban sectors of New Haven. He is a nationally recognized artist (BOLDMINDS Cultural Arts) and author.

In 2002, he founded CTRIBAT Institute for Social Development Inc., which services 210 young males and Females ages nine to 17-years-old. CTRIBAT offers students "life skill" workshops that focus on parent/student participation. The summer pilot called the "Leadership Retreat" focuses on fostering leadership skills in young people who reside in an Urban Environment (At-Risk Youth). The CTRIBAT 2006 Summer Pilot posted an impressive 400% reduction in firearm related violence in the neighborhood of operation. The CTRIBAT runs 12 months year. The program focuses on improving the relationship of law enforcement and the members of the urban sector. In June of 2008, CTRIBAT was awarded the All-American City Award in Tampa Florida.

In January 2007, he was appointed by the Mayor as Coordinator and Program writer of the New Haven Street Outreach Workers Program which is a proactive social development program aimed at reducing violent crime among youth and young adults. With in its first five months of operation, the City of New Haven posted an 86% reduction in homicides. During that two-year period, he served as the Chief Executive Officer for the New Haven Police Department under Police Chief Francisco Ortiz Jr. In June of 2008, the

New Haven Street Outreach Workers Program was awarded the All-American City Award in Tampa Florida.

When asked what was his observation to curing gun-violence? Abdussabur responded, "Having a responsible father who is engaged and aware of his child's past, present and future survival in America."

The results of his works in action are best seen in the historical Dixwell Avenue area or New Haven. Mike Morand, Associate Vice President of Yale University Office of New Haven and State Affairs, coined him as the Nike of urban development. In 2007, he co-founded Omar Ibn Said Leadership Academy Inc. a private boarding school for boy ages eight to 13-years-old that will develop them into global leader. The Omar Academy is the first of its kind in the United States and some leaders has stated that it may be the only one of its kind in the world.

Certification Yale Child Study Fellowship Program, Certification as Instructor Guns is Not Toys Program, TREE Institute-Community Base Police Training, Mentor Certification in New Haven Mentoring Program, Certification as an Instructor for the Eddie Eagle GunSafe Program, NRA Law Enforcement Firearms Instructor, Founder 2ADefense LLC, Public Relations Director for New Haven Mentoring Program Inc., Founder/Executive Director of CTRIBAT Institute for Social Development Inc., Co-Founder and Director of BOLDMINDS Art and Literature LLC, Co-Founder and President of New Haven Guardians Inc., Co Founder/Executive Director Omar Ibn Said Leadership Academy Inc., Board of Director for the Creative Arts Workshop, Founder Eco-Urban Pioneers LLC., Founder Abdussabur LLC, Founder Cyber-Hood Films LLC.

Educational History:
Saint Aedans Elementary School
Graduated Notre Dame High School West Haven
West Georgia College 1985-1989
New Haven Police Academy 1996
Currently enrolled at Charter Oaks Sate College (Public Safety Administration)
2007

Youth Involvement:
Substitute Teacher in New Haven Public Schools 1985-1990
Art Director, Children's Creative Arts Center, New Haven, CT 1991-1993
Behavioral Technician, Area Cooperative Services, Hamden, CT 1991-1994
Executive Director, As We Grow Daycare, New Haven, CT 1994-1996

Other Youth Involvement:
Certification Yale Child Study Fellowship Program
Certification as Instructor Guns is Not Toys Program
TREE Institute-Community Base Police Training
Mentor Certification in New Haven Mentoring Program
Certification as an Instructor for the Eddie Eagle GunSafe Program

Organizational Involvement:
1996 Member of Phi Beta Sigma Fraternity Inc.
1989 Co-Founder and Executive Director of BOLDMINDS Cultural Art Accents
2000 Public Relation Director for New Haven Mentoring Program Inc.
2000 Conservation Firearm Safety Chief Instructor for Connecticut DEP
2002 Founder and Executive Director CTRIBAT Youth Development Program
2002 Founder and Instructor of 2ADFENSE Firearm Safety and Consulting
Agency
2005 Founder Member and President 2004-2008 of New Haven Guardians Inc.
2007 Board of Director Creative Arts Workshop-CAW
2007 Co-Founder and Executive Director Omar Ibin Said Leadership Academy

Other Certifications:
Connecticut POST Certified Police Officer
National Rifle Association Pistol Instructor
National Rifle Association Personal Protection Instructor
National Rifle Association Chief Range Safety Officer Instructor
Member of International Hunter Education Association
National Rifle Association Certified Law Enforcement Firearm Instructor

Awards:
2006 Community Service Award New Haven Public Library
2006 Community Service Award -Phi Beta Sigma Fraternity
2006 Man of the Year- New Haven Independent
2007 Community Service Award-
2007 Man of the Year- Alpha Phi Alpha Fraternity

2008 Man of the Year-National Association of Negro Business & Professional Women's Club, Inc.
2008 Proclamation of the City of New Haven
2008 All American City Award
2008 Nation Drill Team Youth Achievement Award
2009 Proclamation Mayor City of New Haven
2009 Citation New Haven Board of Alderpersons
2009 Declaration Connecticut General Assembly
2009 Letter of Recognition Connecticut Governor Jodi Rell

More Information the Instructor and affiliate programs:
WWW.ABlackmansGuideToLawEnforcementInAmerica.com
WWW.WhyOurChildrenCarryGuns.com
WWW.CTRIBAT.com
WWW.ShafiqAbdussabur.com
WWW.BOLDMINDS.org
WWW.NEWHAVENGUARDIANS.org
WWW.CtUrbanThinkTank.org
WWW.Eco-UrbanPioneers.com

Picture Credits

Front Cover Photo: 2009, BOLDMINDS LLC

Picture #1 pg iii: "Black Anxiety." By Shafiq R. Fulcher Abdussabur
Digital photo design
© BOLDMINDS LLC 2008/ By Shafiq R. Fulcher Abdussabur

Picture #2 pg 1: "Police Car Radio." By Shafiq R. Fulcher Abdussabur
Digital photo
© BOLDMINDS LLC 2006/ By Shafiq R. Fulcher Abdussabur

Picture #3 pg 2: "Alley Lights." By Shafiq R. Fulcher Abdussabur
Digital photo
© BOLDMINDS LLC 2006/ By Shafiq R. Fulcher Abdussabur

Picture #4 pg 22: "The Big House." By Shafiq R. Fulcher Abdussabur
Digital photo
© BOLDMINDS LLC 2006/ By Shafiq R. Fulcher Abdussabur

Picture #5 g 31: "Protect and Serve." 2-10-2000, By Shafiq R. Fulcher Abdussabur
Drawing-Technical Pen, Size: 11"x 14"
© BOLDMINDS LLC 2000/ By Shafiq R. Fulcher Abdussabur

Picture #6 pg 46: "King Me." 2-10-2000, By Shafiq R. Fulcher Abdussabur
Drawing-Technical Pen, Size: 8.5"x 11.5"
© BOLDMINDS LLC 2000/ By Shafiq R. Fulcher Abdussabur

Picture #7 pg 62: "All Aboard." By Shafiq R. Fulcher Abdussabur
Digital photo
© BOLDMINDS LLC 2007/ By Shafiq R. Fulcher Abdussabur

Picture #8 pg 76: "The Paddy Wagon." By Shafiq R. Fulcher Abdussabur

Digital Photograph

© BOLDMINDS LLC 2004/ By Shafiq R. Fulcher Abdussabur

Picture #9 pg 78: Man in jail 12-4-2001, Author Unknown

Digital Photograph, Internet source unknown

Picture #10 pg 90: Photo of Sean Bell's Car.
Digital Photo
Gothamist LLC, Prince Street Station, P.O. Box 510, New York, NY 10012

Picture #11 pg 117: "Lost for Words." By Shafiq R. Fulcher Abdussabur

Drawing-Technical Pen, Size: 11"x 14"

© BOLDMINDS LLC 2000/ By Shafiq R. Fulcher Abdussabur

Picture #12 pg 118: "Shafiq Abdussabur." By Shafiq R. Fulcher Abdussabur

Digital Photo

© NewHavenIndependent.org 2008/ By Allen Appell

Back Cover Photo: "Black Anxiety." By Shafiq R. Fulcher Abdussabur

Digital photo design

© BOLDMINDS LLC 2008/ By Shafiq R. Fulcher Abdussabur

Bibliography

Gomez, Michael Angelo. *Black Crescent: The Experience and Legacy of African Muslims in the Americas.* Illustrated ed. New York: Cambridge University Press, 2005. Print.

..

John Jay College of Criminal Justice
899 Tenth Avenue
New York, NY 10019
Phone: 212-237-8444
Email: mrosen@jjay.cuny.edu

Kats, William Loren. *Eyewitness: The Negro in American History A Living Documentary of the Afro-American Contribution To U.S. History.* 16th Revised ed. New York: Toronto, London: Pitman Publishing Corporation, 1967, 1971. Print.

Law Enforcement News
  Law Enforcement News, a publication of John Jay College of Criminal Justice (CUNY), was published continuously for 30 years beginning in September 1975. The highly acclaimed newspaper, for and about American policing, ceased publication with its September 2005 issue (Vol. XXXI, No. 636).

Star Ledger. George Arwady.

    <http://www.nj.com/starledger/>

Wikimedia: Wikimedia Foundation Inc.
P.O. Box 78350, San Francisco, CA 94107-8350
<_http://en.wikipedia.org/wiki/Abner_Louima>

Wright, Bruce. Black Robes, White Justice: Why Our Legal System Doesn't Work for Blacks. Reprint ed. New York: Kensington Books, 2002. Print.

Man of the Year

"An article from the New Haven Independent online newspaper."

In a year when shootings left New Haveners feeling despair about how to address youth violence, Dixwell beat cop Shafiq Abdussabur offered inspiration. How he got to be a cop — and in a position to make a difference—offers another inspiring tale, about how to build a true "community policing" force.

The 39-year-old former high-school track star patrols Dixwell, the neighborhood where he grew up. He saw up close how younger and younger kids were increasingly using guns to settle disputes. He saw the

impact it was having on families. He saw how little kids had to do. So, on his off hours he started a program for young teens he saw at risk of being lured into long-term trouble. He took them camping. He brought them to jail, too. He invited cops and former gang-bangers and addicts for lessons about real life.

This year the program took off; fifty-five boys spent the summer in Abdussabur's CTRIBAT program. And they stayed out of trouble. Their stretch of town stayed quieter than other crime-plagued neighborhoods. By year's end, the whole city noticed. The city government and other major institutions came through with money to expand CTRIBAT; a new program teaching teens video is starting up at the Stetson Branch Library.

The big picture: Yes, you can reach kids from tough homes in tough neighborhoods, You can make their lives, and the whole city, safer.

Abdussabur's initiative is a textbook case of community policing, of cops who know their neighborhoods, who know the people in them, who work with other groups on solutions that don't require arresting people.

Abdussabur's route to becoming a cop, on the other hand, is anything but a classic case. Entrepreneur, artist, activist protesting the cops — people fitting those descriptions don't usually end up wearing the badge.

Maybe, as New Haven recruits new cops and struggles to return to the roots of its community policing effort, it may consider returning to such unconventional ideas about who's part of "us" and who's part of "them."

Mom Was A Panther
Abdussabur's earliest view of activists and cops came from the shoulders of his mother's friend.

Abdussabur — his name then was Tommy Fulcher Johnson — couldn't have been older then four or five. His mom, Brenda Johnson, took him to the Green for a Black Panther rally. She worked as an aide in the public schools. She also belonged to the Panthers, a group calling for armed revolution in America.

"I remember being hoisted upon [her friend's] shoulders and seeing all these leather hats and jackets — like I have on now, only black — and seeing all these cops lined up with German shepherds," Abdussabur recalled in a conversation at his unofficial Church Street office, Willoughby's coffee shop.

He still visibly recalled the tension he felt as police charged at the protesters. His mother grabbed him, and they took off. "We ran from the mall all the way to Edgar Street," their home in the Hill. Abdussabur remembered sitting with his mom on their front porch later that afternoon. He remembered the tension, again, as a cop drove by, "in slow motion, definitely looking."

The family moved to Florence Virtue Homes in Dixwell, where Abdussabur spent most of his childhood. He went to St. Aedan's parochial school. Afternoons were spent at grandma's (mom and dad, a postal employee, were working) or with friends drawing pictures from books at Stetson on Dixwell Avenue. Abdussabur said he'd get in a little trouble at school, but not much. He blossomed at Notre Dame High School, where he made all-state on the track team and won a state Congressional Art Award for an acrylic painting.

That award won him a full scholarship to the Rhode Island School of Design. But he chose instead to accept a track scholarship to The University of West Georgia in Carrollton, Georgia, where he studied architecture, interior design, and philosophy.

Schooled in Real Life

In his freshman year at the largely white Southern school (University of West Georgia), Abdussabur found himself selected as president of the Black Student Alliance. He also became head of a black fraternity (Phi Beta Sigma), and organized the first joint Greek Week involving white and black fraternities. Brenda Johnson's son was finding his voice.

"I started getting called to the dean's office. He wanted to know what would make a 'Yankee come down to be so concerned about what was happening down here.'"

He continued butting heads with the administration over unspent budgeted money for the alliance, then over a shantytown he organized to protest the school's investments in apartheid South Africa. White students were joining in the protest. The president asked Abdussabur to remove the structure, since the school was simultaneously holding an open house for prospective students.

"If you give me a letter that you're willing to divest, we'll take it down," Abdussabur replied.

No deal! The protests continued. Cops started hassaling the protesters. Weeks later, the school divested from South Africa.

And a black administrator called Abdussabur in for a chat. "I'll never forget it. He said, 'When you've got your hand in the lion's mouth, be careful not to tickle his palate.'"

On a trip back home, Abdussabur hooked up with activist Scot X Esdaile and started attending a Nation of Islam mosque in Bridgeport. "I was searching for religion. I had studied black history. I had on the Malcolm X overcoat, the hat, the bowtie."

Soon after, in his junior year, Abdussabur's paperwork for his scholarship mysteriously went "missing." When the office found them, it was too late, he was told, for him to qualify for the money. He had no dough to stay in school.

BOLDMINDS

He invested some of his last $400 in equipment to carve wood medallions with nationalist themes — "Africa, Nefertiti heads. He formed a company called BOLDMINDS to sell the medallions. Within three years, traveling in the south and on the East Coast, he sold 10,000 pieces.

He also traveled to Atlanta, where he served in a police job of sorts — the Fruit of Islam, the Nation's stone faced security force.

He was also traveling back home, where his mom was ill. He eventually settled back in New Haven. And he decided to leave the Nation of Islam. "I was trying to find a religion that did not make color a factor," he recalled. "No matter how you sliced it, NOI, color was a central factor. In Georgia, [many of] my allies and mentors were white."

One day he attended a fund-raiser for New Haven's Masjid al-Islam, which is affiliated with Orthodox Sunni Islam.

"I saw all these Indians and Pakistanis and African-Americans and white people. I said, 'There's going to be a fight!'

"I look at the door. There was no security!

"I was amazed — all these people could be in a room, different cultures, eating together." Abdussabur was sold.

He joined up with the masjid. He adopted his current name: Shafiq, for "compassionate," and Abdussabur, for "servant of God."

The members of the George Street masjid, near the Hospital of St. Raphael, noticed that their neighbors on nearby Greenwood Street were basically living hostage to drug dealers on their block. They couldn't get the cops to take action. So Abdussabur and other masjid members formed their own patrols to confront the dealers head on. They also confronted the cops, protesting their lack of response.

Abdussabur further confronted the cops, publicly, when he and activist Michael Jefferson formed an All-Civilian Review Board to monitor police brutality. It was the mid-'90s, the dawn of community policing in New Haven, when then-Chief Nicholas Pastore was looking in unusual places — gay and lesbians newspapers, universities, black and Hispanic publications — to build a force built on a new model. Pastore called Abdussabur in for a chat. "Why don't you become a cop?" he suggested.

A Deserted "Ave."

Abdussabur took the suggestion. He's glad he did. He likes patrolling his old neighborhood.

He's also busy outside of patrol, selling his artwork, organizing his youth program. He lives in Beaver Hills with his wife, Mubarakah Ibrahim, and their four children. They remain active in the George Street masjid. Abdussabur prays five times a day. A gregarious man prone to big-grin outbursts, he never stops running, or cooking up new projects.

Closest to his heart is CTRIBAT Institute for Social Development, which in his view is part of being a cop.

He recalled a camping trip to Rock Neck State Park with his kids in late July. "I kept asking myself: Is this campaign thing working?"

One of the boys had been known to carry guns in the neighborhood; his family was in and out of jail. "I overheard him talking to another of the young boys: 'I like this. I don't never wanna go back home. The Tribe (neighborhood gang faction of the "Bloods") is corny. All we do is go to the store and hang out on the Ave. Go to the store, hang out on the Ave.'" (The boy signed up for an after-school football program this fall and has stayed out of trouble, according to Abdussabur.)

The trip ended with Abdussabur and the kids pulling into Dixwell in a borrowed Police Athletic League van around 3 p.m. "It had to be 97 degrees. They said, 'Shafiq, drive by the Ave.' I said, 'Can't you guys give it up?'"

He thought they wanted to show off for their friends hanging out at Dixwell Plaza. He drove by, reluctantly. "They said, 'Where everybody at?' Nobody was hanging out. I said, 'Because you're all in the car.'"

That's when Abdussabur knew: "We had 'em." The "root element" wasn't hanging out.

BY PAUL BASS Founder/Editor
www.NewHavenIndependent.com

DECEMBER 21, 2006 12:31

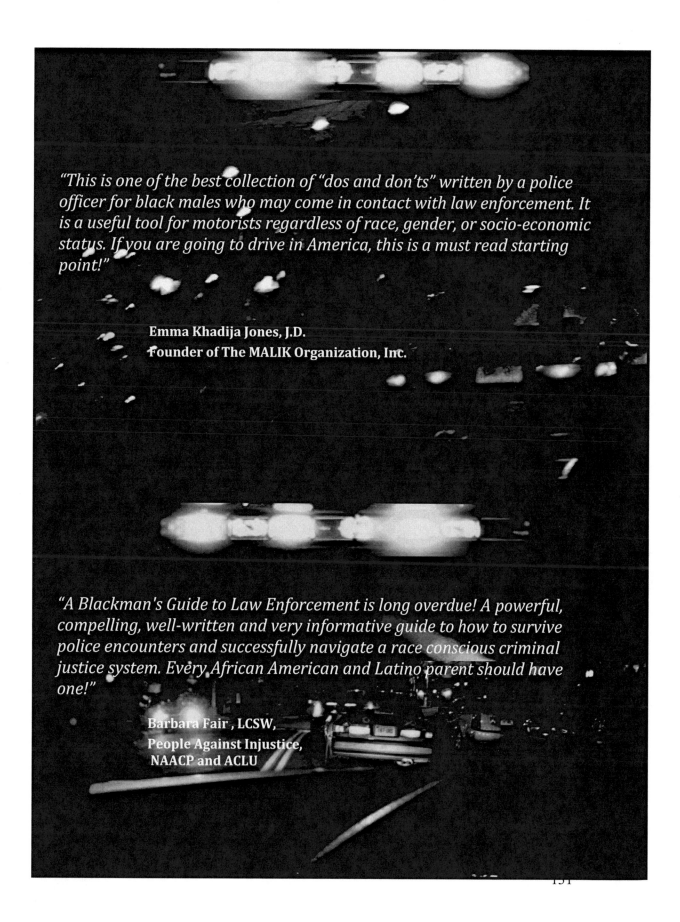

"This is one of the best collection of "dos and don'ts" written by a police officer for black males who may come in contact with law enforcement. It is a useful tool for motorists regardless of race, gender, or socio-economic status. If you are going to drive in America, this is a must read starting point!"

Emma Khadija Jones, J.D.
Founder of The MALIK Organization, Inc.

"A Blackman's Guide to Law Enforcement is long overdue! A powerful, compelling, well-written and very informative guide to how to survive police encounters and successfully navigate a race conscious criminal justice system. Every African American and Latino parent should have one!"

Barbara Fair , LCSW,
People Against Injustice,
NAACP and ACLU

CPSIA information can be obtained at www.ICGtesting.com
260214BV00003B/1-100/P